Soyons heureux !
O Be Joyful!

A Bahá'í Songbook

Ruth Vander Stelt

This book is dedicated to Glenn Cameron whose enthusiasm and love for the Funds of the Cause have been a model of inspiration.

"singing and music are the spiritual food of the hearts and souls."

Bahá'u'lláh, according to 'Abdu'l-Bahá, in Bahá'í World Faith.

Mille merci à Josée Cardinal, pour son expertise musicale et son soutien extraordinaire. Many thanks to my one and only, Patrick Marshall, for his musical support and consistent encouragement.

Soyons heureux !
O Be Joyful!
A Bahá'í Songbook

Ruth Vander Stelt

Soyons heureux !
O Be Joyful!
A Bahá'í Songbook
Ruth Vander Stelt

Distributed by White Mountain Publications
Box 5180, New Liskeard, ON P0J 1P0
www.wmpub.ca

National Library of Canada Cataloguing in Publication

Soyons heureux! [music] = O Be Joyful! : a Bahá'í Songbook / Ruth Vander Stelt.

Melodies and lyrics, with chord symbols for guitar.
Includes songs in English, French and Arabic.

ISBN 1-894747-04-6

1. Bahai Faith—Songs and music. I. Vander Stelt, Ruth, 1963- II. Title: O Be Joyful!
III. Title: Bahá'í Songbook.

M2145.B34S732 2003 782.25 C2003-903052-0

Please do not photocopy. Your purchase of this songbook will directly contribute to the Lifeblood of the Cause through the National Spiritual Assembly of the Bahá'ís of Canada.

Cover and book design by Del Carry

Printed by National Printers

Printed in Canada

Submissions for future editions of this compilation may be made to:

Ruth Vander Stelt
c/o Spiritual Assembly of the Bahá'ís of Gatineau
C.P. 79033, Galeries de Hull
Gatineau, Québec, J8Y 6V2

Contents

# *Introduction*

My daughter's eyes opened wide in awe.
"I think I saw one, Maman! "
"One what, dear? "
"An angel! I'm sure I saw one! When I was opening my eyes after my prayer, and they were just less than half open, I'm sure I saw an angel flying through my room and out the door! "
My face softened in a smile.
"And what do you think she was doing? "
"Well, she was taking my prayer away to the other people in the world, just like it says in the writing, remember? "

> "Intone, O My servant, the verses of God
> that have been received by thee,
> as intoned by them who have drawn
> nigh unto Him,
> that the sweetness of thy melody
> may kindle thine own soul,
> and attract the hearts of all men.
> Whoso reciteth, in the privacy of his chamber,
> the verses revealed by God,
> the scattering angels of the Almighty
> shall scatter abroad the fragrance
> of the words uttered by his mouth,
> and shall cause the heart
> of every righteous man to throb.
> Though he may, at first, remain unaware
> of its effect, yet the virtue
> of the grace vouchsafed unto him
> must needs sooner or later exercise
> its influence upon his soul.
> Thus have the mysteries of the Revelation
> of God been decreed
> by virtue of the Will of Him
> Who is the Source of power and wisdom."

— Bahá'u'lláh

Words cannot express the joy I have had compiling the First Edition of this songbook. From children's classes to Feasts and other Bahá'í gatherings, to e-mail and the Internet, I have gathered together songs that resonate with the depths and the nuances of the Bahá'í writings and teachings.

This endeavour to systematize part of the arts for distribution to the larger community has been the unfolding and blossoming of one of the most beautiful flowers we could possibly offer to the present Bahá'í world.

Indeed, the primary goal of Soyons heureux! O Be Joyful! is to provide a resource for individual and group singing at children's classes, Feasts, and other gatherings.

Songwriters and contributors around the world have happily given me permission to publish their songs which will now be known and sung by many people desirous of kindling their souls with the sweetness of their melodies. In a few cases, however, it has not been possible to ascertain author identification.

Users of this songbook will note that songs and chants have been chosen, above all, for their accessibility to learning. In this regard, consideration has been given to both length of song and language. Although not every language of every ethnic group is represented, this first edition does reflect Canada's linguistic diversity.

The guitar chords have been adjusted for ease of play, with a capo being used on the more difficult-to-play keys. The more experienced player may prefer to play the songs in their original key, written in simple letters without the fret board indication, to the right of the capoed chord. Bass chords (ex. A/E, where A is the chord played, and E is the bass chord), are not obligatory.

We have already begun work on the Second Edition of this book. Once again, we invite the international community of songwriters and contributors to participate in its elaboration. Entries should include identification of composer, his/her coordinates, source of text, year of composition, melody line or full score if available, guitar chords, lyrics, permission to publish and distribute the song, and an audio reference if available. Especially welcome for the second edition are songs about the early history of the Bahá'í Faith, its principles and symbols, and occasional songs related to Holy Days and specific Feasts. For aspiring composers of song - anyone who has ever hummed, whistled, or sung a tune - record yourself, even if it's in the simplest of ways, and ask a friend with some basic music theory to write it out for you. It is important to know that many of the songs in the present edition were originally oral; they had not been written down until now. Unwritten, even when transmitted from one singer to another, many wonderful songs have been lost over time; those that are still in circulation may suffer the same fate.

Comments on and corrections to this first edition of Soyons Heureux! O Be Joyful! as well as any information on the composers of the few songs I have not been able to identify, are welcome and should be sent through the Local Spiritual Assembly of the Bahá'ís of Gatineau, C.P. 79033, Gatineau, Québec, J8Y 6V2.

It is my hope that those of you who purchase this book use it to its fullest. You are asked however, not to photocopy any part of it. The bottom of every page carries this message which is a courtesy to you. With all profit going to the Lifeblood of the Cause, you may be assured that the fruits of your effort, channeled through contribution to the Fund as well as through full use of the songbook, will be plentiful.

In the words of 'Abdu'l-Bahá, "Work, work with all your strength, spread the cause of the kingdom… "!

Yá Bahá'u'l-Abhá!

Ruth Vander Stelt, M.D.

A Place in the Choir

Text and Music: Bill Staines, 1978

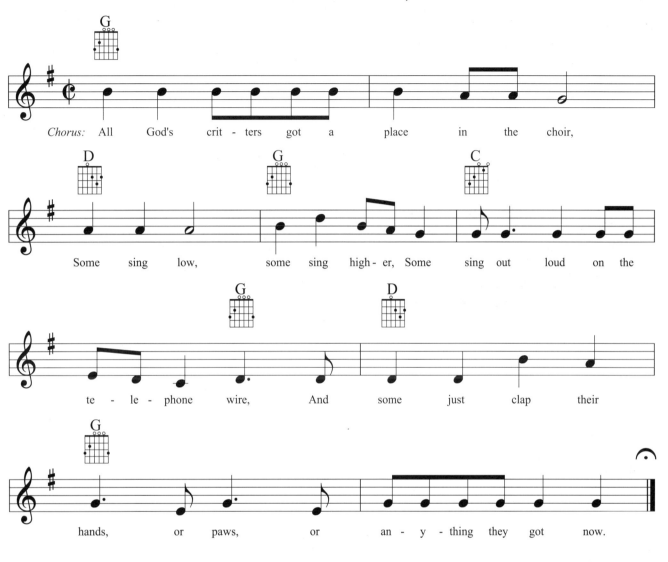

Chorus: All God's crit - ters got a place in the choir,

Some sing low, some sing high - er, Some sing out loud on the

te - le - phone wire, And some just clap their

hands, or paws, or an - y - thing they got now.

Aie le cœur pur

Text: Bahá'u'lláh, Hidden Words No. 1 and No. 59 (Arabic)
Paroles : Bahá'u'lláh, *Les Paroles Cachées, n° 1 et n° 59 (en arabe)*
Music/Musique : Chantal Daigle, 1993

L'art de la musique est divin et produit un grand effet. C'est la nourriture de l'âme et de l'esprit.

Sélections des écrits d'Abdu'l-Bahá

Alláh'u'Abhá - 95 times

Sing 5 times to total 95 Alláh'u'Abhás
Text: Incantation ordained in the Most Holy Book, the Kitáb-i-Aqdas
Meaning "God is All-Glorious"
Music: Josée Cardinal, 2000

Alláh'u'Abhá (French – en français)

Suggestion: take turns having one child sing the short phrases,
with everyone singing the Alláh'u'Abhá's
Suggestion: À tour de rôle, demandez aux enfants de chanter les courtes phrases
alors que le groupe chantera les 'Alláh'u'Abhá.'
Text and Music/Paroles et musique: Suzanne Hébert, 1986

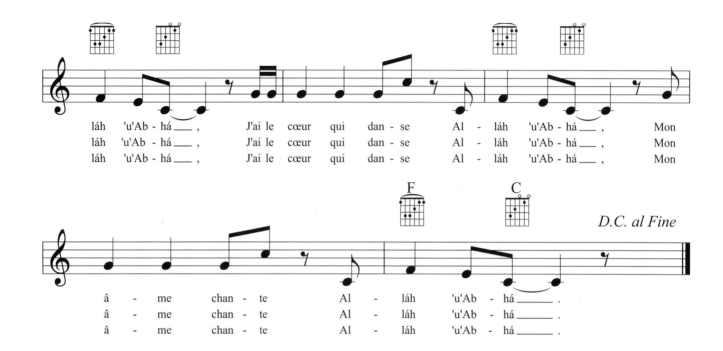

láh 'u'Ab - há ____ , J'ai le cœur qui dan - se Al - láh 'u'Ab - há ____ , Mon
láh 'u'Ab - há ____ , J'ai le cœur qui dan - se Al - láh 'u'Ab - há ____ , Mon
láh 'u'Ab - há ____ , J'ai le cœur qui dan - se Al - láh 'u'Ab - há ____ , Mon

D.C. al Fine

â - me chan - te Al - láh 'u'Ab - há ____ .
â - me chan - te Al - láh 'u'Ab - há ____ .
â - me chan - te Al - láh 'u'Ab - há ____ .

Alláh'u'Abhá, My Name is...

In French, sing "Alláh'u'Abhá, Mon nom est ...."
En français, chanter «Alláh'u'Abhá, Mon nom est ... »
Text and Music/Paroles et musique: Josée Cardinal, 1999

Nom comptant une syllabe
Name with one syllable

Al - láh 'u'Ab - há My name is .... Al -

láh 'u'Ab - há My name is ....

Nom comptant deux syllabes
Name with two syllables

Al - láh 'u'Ab - há My name is ... ... Al -

láh 'u'Ab - há My name is ... ...

MY NAME IS...
MON NOM EST...

17

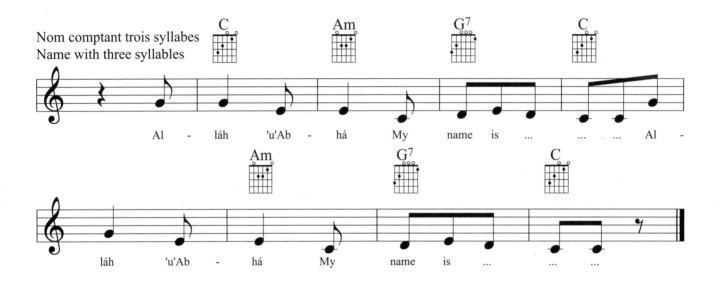

Nom comptant trois syllabes
Name with three syllables

Al - láh 'u'Ab - há My name is ... ... Al -

láh 'u'Ab - há My name is ... ...

The diversity in the human family should be the cause of love and harmony, as it is in music where many different notes blend together in the making of a perfect chord.

'Abdu'l-Bahá, Paris Talks

Alláhuma Yá Subbúh, Yá Quddús

Text: the Báb, Bahá'u'lláh
Music: Bijan Khadem-Missagh, 1980
see Arabic pronunciation key

Al - lá - hum - ma   yá   sub - bú - hu   yá   qud - dús

yá   han - ná - nu   yá - man - nán   Far - rij   la - ná

bil   faz - li   val   ih - sán ___   in - na - ka   rah - mán - un   man - nán

in - na - ka   rah - mán - un   man - nán   Ba -

Fine

English Paraphrase

Our God, who is compassionate and pure,
Assist us through Your mercy and kindness.
Remove our difficulties with bounties and
generosity

Animals

Text and Music: Wiley Rinaldi, 1983

Chorus: Ya ta da ta da ta da ta da ta

da

1. Snort! Snort!
2. Arf! Arf!
3. Meeooow!
4. Moooooo!

Ya ta da

Quack! Quack! Quack! Quack! Quack!

no guitar this bar

1. The crea-tures in this big world, whe-ther they walk or
2. The don-key car-ries his bur-den, the kit-ty purrs in our
3. The dog on our front door-step, he is our faith-ful

fly, or fly, are part of one cre-a-tion _____
lap, our lap_____, and the birds sing sweet-ly _____
friend, our friend; we al-so thank our milk cow_____

21

From every part of the moutain the symphony of "Yá Bahá'u'l-Abhá!"
will be raised, and before the daybreak soul-entrancing music accompanied
by melodious voices will be uplifted towards the throne of the Almighty.

'Abdu'l-Bahá in Bahá'u'lláh and the New Era, by J.E. Esslemont

Ayyám-i-Há

Text and Music: Joyce and Danny Deardorff, 1975

Bass guitar chords may be left out if desired

Capo 1st Fret

I will buy you a
I will bake you some

pre - sent____, and you will bake me a pie, Then we'll o - pen the
cook - ies____, and you will paint them_ bright, to ce - le - brate spring's

pre__ -sents____ and get all sta - rry eyed. Then we'll stand a -
com__ -ing____, to melt the snow and ice. Then we'll stand a -

round the ring, all hol - ding hands for Ay -
round the ring, all hol - ding hands for Ay -

23

yám - i - Há's the gift of God to man ____

yám - i - Há's the gift of God to man ____

____ . Ay - yam - i - Há ____ , the gift of God to

man ____ , and in the spi - rit of His gi ____ -ving, we

try to un - der - stand ____ : Ay - yám - i - Há's the

gift of God to man ____ .

Bahá'í Lullaby

Text and Music: Jim Styan, 1981

Softly

Sleep, ba - by, sleep in the bo - som of His love. Rest, ba - by, rest in His

most lo - ving arms. Peace- ful and calm, con - ten - ted and sure,

you will be loved for - ev - er_____ more _____ .

Sleep, ba - by, sleep in the breast of His grace. Rest, ba - by, rest in the

cra - dle of His care. Gen - tle and qui - et, rare and so true, the

Fine

Lord of all worlds is watch - ing o - ver you _____ .

Feel the warm breez -es of His gifts ne - ver end - ing. Par - take of His fa- vours, so

D.C. al Fine

sweet and con - firm - ing, real trea - sures find - ing you.

Bahá'ís We Are

Text and Music: Ariel Barkley, 1986

Ba - ha'is we are Ba - ha'is we are Ba - ha'is we are Ba - ha'is we are First came the Báb and the Báb means the Gate, Then came Ba - há - 'u' - lláh, the Found - er of the

---

The art of music must be brought to the highest stage of development, for this is one of the most wonderful arts and in this glorious age of the Lord of Unity it is highly essential to gain its mastery.

Extract from an untranslated Tablet by 'Abdu'l-Bahá

27

Faith, Fol - lowed by 'Ab - du'l - Ba - há, the

Cen - tre of the Co - ve - nant and Sho - ghi Ef -

fen - di, the Guar - dian of the Cause ____ . Ba - ha'is we are Ba -

ha'is we are Ba - ha'is we are Ba - ha'is ____ .

Be on Fire with the Love of the Kingdom

A rythmic chant in three parts.
A first group begins with the first part, putting the emphasis on the words in bold.
A second group contributes the second part, with a whole rest on the last bar.
A third group or individual sings the third part.
To be chanted either a definite or an indefinite amount of times.
Text and Rythm: Alfred Côté, 1995

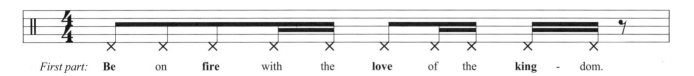

First part: **Be** on **fire** with the **love** of the **king** - dom.

Be on **fire** with the **love** of the **king** - dom. **Be** on **fire** with the **love** of the **king** - dom.

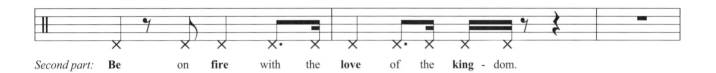

Second part: **Be** on **fire** with the **love** of the **king** - dom.

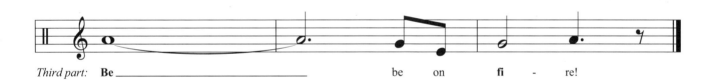

Third part: **Be** _____ be on fi - re!

Béni est le lieu

Text/Paroles : Bahá'u'lláh
Music/Musique: Suzanne Hébert, 1986

Bé - ni est le lieu, et la mai - son, et l'en -

droit _____ , et la _____ ville, et le _____

cœur, et la mon - ta - gne _____ , et le re -

fuge, et la ca - verne, et la val - lée, et le pa -

J'espère...que le drapeau de l'unité du monde de l'humanité soit déployé, que la mélodie de la Paix universelle parvienne aux oreilles de l'Orient de l'Occident.

'Abdu'l-Bahá, Les tablettes du plan divin

Blessed is the Spot

Text: Bahá'u'lláh
Music: Elizabeth Hahn, 1974

At the outset of every endeavour, it is incumbent to look to the end of it. Of all the arts and sciences, set the children to studying those which will result in advantage to man, will ensure his progress and elevate his rank. Thus the noisome odours of lawlessness will be dispelled, and thus through the high endeavours of the nation's leaders, all will live cradled, secure and in peace.

From Lawh-i- Maqsúd, Tablets of Bahá'u'lláh
Revealed After the Kitáb-i-Aqdas

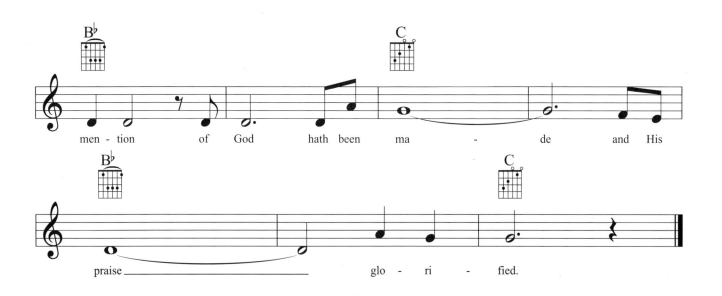

men - tion of God hath been ma - de and His

praise _____ glo - ri - fied.

Blessing and Peace

Text: excerpt from the Medium Obligatory Prayer, Bahá'u'lláh
Music: Ruth Vander Stelt, 2000

Bles- sing___ and peace, sa - lu - ta - tion___ and glo - ry, rest up - on Thy

loved ones, whom the chan - ges and the chan - ces of the world have not de - terred from

turn - ing un - to Thee, and who've gi - ven___ their all, in the

hope of___ ob - tai - ning that which is with Thee.

Brand New Words

Text and Music: Dick Grover, 1970

"The unofficial school song at the New Era Bahá'í School in India in the 1970's"

1. In Ja - pan, in Swi - tzer - land, Pe - ru, and Zan - zi - bar, with
2. The world is but one coun - try, we're learn - ing this to - day. And
3. We have all been li - kened to leaves up - on one tree, ---
4. Make the na - tions one, let re - li - gions all a - gree. Be

bon - goes and ma - rim - bas, ban - joes and gui - tar,
all man - kind its ci - ti - zens, these words will show the way.
flo - wers in one gar - den, waves up - on one sea,
oc - cu - pied with ser - vice to all hu - man - i - ty.

Peo - ple are sing - ing, have - n't you heard? A
For all of us to ful - ly learn our ta - lents and worth, so
Bril - liant shin - ing stars, ra - diant can - dles, rays of light, ---
No - thing less than u - ni - ty can sa - tis - fy our minds, So

new day is dawn - ing, we have brand new words.
we can build a new world or - der here on earth.
birds sing - ing in the gar - den day and night.
tell the world a - bout the one - ness of man - kind.

Build a New House

Text and Music: Dick Grover, 1988

Chorus: Sing this me - lo - dy, build a new house with me.

Yes - ter - day is rolled up and gone, there's a new day rea - dy to dawn.

1. My black bro - ther's un - hap - py _____ , made to
2. My yel - low sis - ter is hun - gry _____ , though she
3. My red sis - ter is si - lent _____ , speak - ing
4. My white bro - ther is fear - ful _____ of a
5. All my rain ____ - bow re - la - tives _____ are ____

live on a few cer - tain streets, But we'll
works in the fields all _____ day, In _____
her grief ____ with her _____ eyes. To _____ -
change that he knows must _____ come, But when
buil - ding a house that's _____ new, And _____

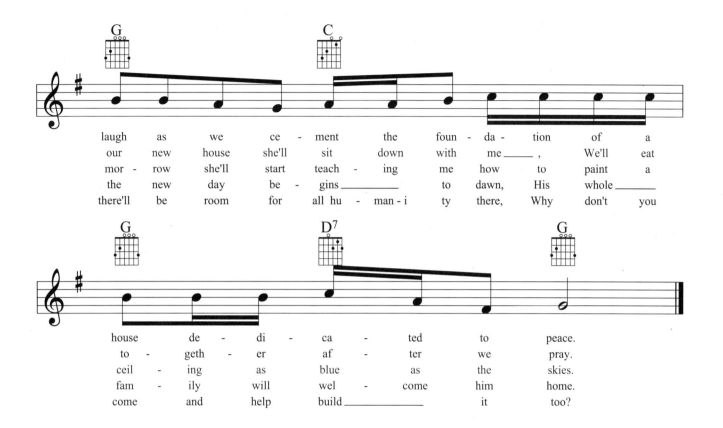

laugh	as	we	ce -	ment	the	foun -	da -	tion	of	a
our	new	house	she'll	sit	down	with	me _____ ,	We'll	eat
mor -	row	she'll	start	teach -	ing	me	how	to	paint	a
the	new	day	be -	gins _____		to	dawn,	His	whole _____
there'll	be	room	for	all	hu -	man - i	ty	there,	Why	don't	you

house	de -	di -	ca -	ted	to	peace.
to -	geth -	er	af -	ter	we	pray.
ceil -	ing	as	blue	as	the	skies.
fam -	ily	will	wel -	come	him	home.
come	and	help	build _____		it	too?

The art of music is divine and effective … It has wonderful sway and effect in the hearts of children, for their hearts are pure and melodies have great influence in them.

A Compilation on Bahá'í Education,
Research Department of the Universal House of Justice

Children of God (La foi bahá'íe)

May be sung as a two, three, or four-part round.
Peut être chanté en canon en deux, trois, ou quatre voix, comme l'indiquent les nombres.
French version below - Version française ci-dessous
Arrangement: Ruth Vander Stelt, 1999
Text and music/Paroles et musique : ?

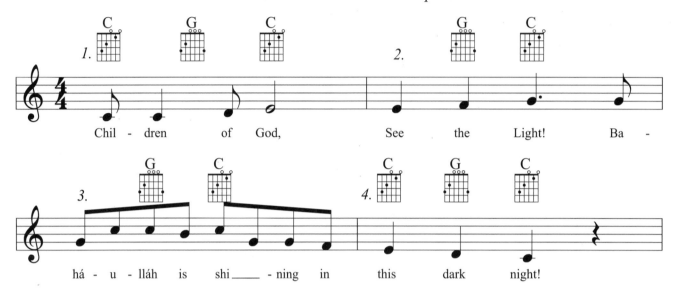

Chil - dren of God, See the Light! Ba -
há - u - lláh is shi____ - ning in this dark night!

La foi bahá'íe

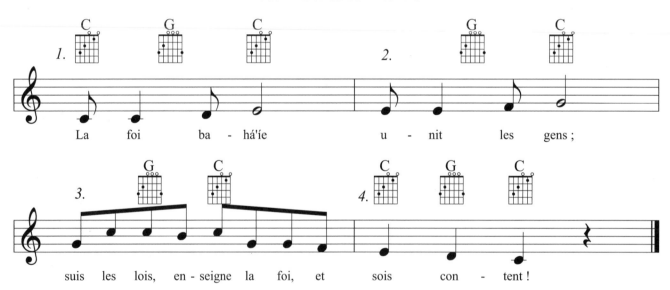

La foi ba - há'íe u - nit les gens ;
suis les lois, en - seigne la foi, et sois con - tent !

Close One Eye

call-response based on Hidden Word No. 12 (Persian)
Arrangement: Ruth Vander Stelt, 1999

One person leads, speaking the lines in a rhythmic fashion while making the indicated gestures.
All others repeat the lines and gestures immediately after the leader.

Call:	We-ll!
Gesture:	left hand on left hip for "we-"
	right hand on right hip for "-ll."
Call:	You gotta close one eye
Gesture:	covers right eye
Call:	and open the other!
Gesture:	opens left eye wide between thumb and index
Call:	ou gotta close one eye
Gesture:	take thumb and index off left eye, leaving right eye covered
Call:	to the world outside
Gesture:	leave right eye covered, and make sweeping action, palm up, in a semi-circle,
	as if to keep something away
Call:	and open the other
Gesture:	open left eye between thumb and index
Call:	open r-e-a-l wide!
Gesture:	open left eye even wider, and look all around while leaning forward
Call:	and take a look around
Gesture:	left hand on forehead, scanning the horizon, both eyes open
Call:	at the beauty we've found!
Gesture:	both hands, palms up, together in front, then moving outwards, showing the surroundings
Call:	It's Bahá'u'lláh
Gesture:	arms up in the air
Call:	Who brings us all here
Gesture:	both hands, palms up, together in front, then moving outwards, showing
	everyone in the room
Call:	It's Bahá'u'lláh
Gesture:	arms up in the air
Call:	who makes us all cheer!
Gesture:	clap to the beat of the words: once on "makes" and once on "cheer"

ALL TOGETHER, *hands in the air:* "YEAH!"

39

Courtesy

Text and Music: Nancy Ward, 1985

1. Cour - te - sy is grea - ter than the rays of the sun. Cour - te - sy is grea - ter than the rays, than the rays of the sun.
2. Man - ners are a gift _____ that we give to eve - ry - one. Man - ners are a gift _____ , that we give, that we give to eve - ry - one.
3. Love _____ is the best thing that we hold in our hearts. Love _____ is the best thing that we hold, that we hold in our hearts.

Optional section after 3 verses

Truth _____ , truth is a light that

Repeat Courtesy verse

Dis : Dieu suffit à tout

French version of "Say God Sufficeth"
May be sung as a four part round, as numbers indicate
Peut être chanté comme un canon à quatre voix, comme l'indiquent les nombres
Text: the Báb / Paroles : Le Báb
Music/Musique : Tom Price, 1972

Dis : Dieu suf - fit à tout, au des - sus de tout.

Rien, ni dans les cieux, ni sur la terre, sauf Dieu ne peut

suf - fire. En vé - ri - té, il est en lui - même, Ce -

lui qui sait, Ce - lui qui sou - tient, l'Om - ni - po - tent.

Dis la vérité

Text/Paroles : Bahá'u'lláh, in *L'art divin de vivre*
Music/Musique : Chantal Daigle, 1993

1. Quand tu dis la vé - ri - té ___ tu gagnes la con -
2. Quand tu dis la vé - ri - té ___ tu se - ras très
3. Si tu mens on te blâ - me - ra ___ et tu peux perdre
4. Yá Ba - há - 'u'l - Ab ___ - há Yá Ba - há - 'u'l -

fiance des gens ___ , dis tou - jours la vé - ri - té ___ ,
fière de toi ___ , Dieu se - ra con - tent de toi ___ ,
tes a - mis ___ , Que ta langue soit vé - ri - dique,
Ab ___ - há ___ , Yá Ba - há - 'u'l - Ab ___ - há ___ ,

Yá Ba - há - 'u'l - Ab - há ___ . La vé - ra - ci - té
Yá Ba - há - 'u'l - Ab - há ___ .
Yá Ba - há - 'u'l - Ab - há ___ .
Yá Ba - há - 'u'l - Ab - há ___ .

est le fon ___ - de - ment de toutes les ver - tus hu - mai - nes ;

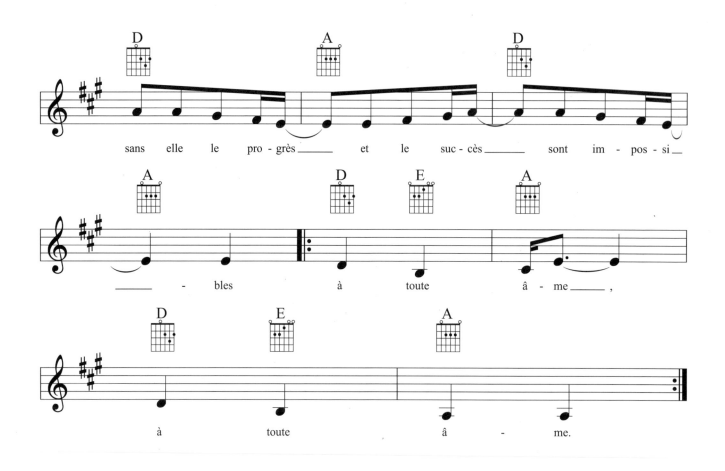

sans elle le pro - grès _____ et le suc - cès _____ sont im - pos - si _____

_____ - bles   à   toute   â - me _____ ,

à   toute   â - me.

Fermer un œil

Chanson à répondre basée sur la Parole Cachée n° 12 en persan
Arrangements: Ruth Vander Stelt, 1999

L'animateur entame ce chant de façon rythmique, tout en faisant les gestes indiqués ; tous répondent immédiatement avec les mêmes paroles et gestes.

Chant: Eh bien!

Geste: Poser la main gauche sur la hanche gauche pour le « Eh »
    Poser la main droite sur la hanche droite pour le « bien »

Chant: Il faut fermer un œil

Geste: couvrir l'œil droit avec la main droite

Chant: et ouvrir l'autre!

Geste: ouvrir l'œil gauche entre l'index et le pouce gauche

Chant: il faut fermer un œil

Geste: découvrir l'œil gauche, tout en gardant l'œil droit couvert

Chant: au monde extérieur

Geste: garder l'œil droit couvert et balayer le bras gauche devant soi, paume levée, comme si l'on voulait empêcher quelqu'un de s'approcher

Chant: et ouvrir l'autre

Geste: ouvrir l'œil gauche entre le pouce et l'index

Chant: l'ouvrir t-r-è-s grand

Geste: ouvrir l'œil gauche encore plus grand, se pencher vers l'avant, et regarder tout autour de soi

Chant: et regarder tout partout

Geste: placer la main gauche au front, les deux yeux ouverts, et examiner tout l'horizon

Chant: la beauté près de nous!

Geste: placer les deux mains ensemble devant soi, paumes levées, et les ouvrir vers l'extérieur, en montrant les environs

Chant: C'est Bahá'u'lláh

Geste: lever les bras au-dessus de la tête

Chant: qui veut nous réunir

Geste: placer les deux mains ensemble devant soi, paumes levées, et les ouvrir vers l'extérieur, en montrant tous les gens réunis

Chant: C'est Bahá'u'lláh

Geste: lever les bras au-dessus de la tête

Chant: qui nous fait applaudir !

Geste: taper des mains au rythme du chant, soit une fois sur « fait » et une fois sur « -dir »

TOUS ENSEMBLE, LES MAINS LEVÉES : « YEAH ! »

First Thing

Text and Music: Jim Styan, 1996

1. When you wake up in the mor - ning ____ , it is
2. When you wake up in the mor - ning ____ , it is
4. When you wake up in the mor - ning ____ , it is
5. When you wake up in the mor - ning ____ , say: "What

good to say your prayers, first thing _____
good to turn to God, first thing _____
good to wash your face first thing _____
tongue can voice my thanks to Thee to - day _____

___ . When you get up in the mor - ning, it is
___ . When you get up in the mor - ning, it is
___ . When you get up in the mor - ning, it is
___ , When you get up in the mor - ning, say: "All

good to see God's beau - ty, a - ris - ing _____
good to feel the love _____ He _____ brings _____
good to touch your soul, in - spi _____ - ring _____
praise be un - to God in ev - ery way." _____

46

—,   em - brace   Him_____.   When   you
—.   and   I   sing_____.   When   you
—,   like   a   spring_____.   When   you
____   and   I   say_____.   When   you

F   **C**

gaze   out   on   the   lake   of   life   re - freshed   at   ros - y
look   out   on   the   beau - ty____   of   all   God's   cre - a -
pu - ri - fy   your   bo - dy   with   clean   water   and   rose   fra -
pray   for   your   dear   pa - rents____,   great   bless - ings   you   will

F

dawn,   You'll   learn   the   mys - tic   me - lo - dies,   re -
tion   You'll   see   the   sun   is   shi - ning____   in the
grance,   you'll re - joice   the   soul   in   pa - ra - dise   as the   ve -
see.   O - bey   them,   show   them   kind - ness____,   give them

G   *Fine*

flect - ing   in   its   calm_____.   3. O   God,
heart   of   all   mor - nings_____.
ry   es-sence   of clean - li - ness_____.
love   and   cha - ri - ty_____.

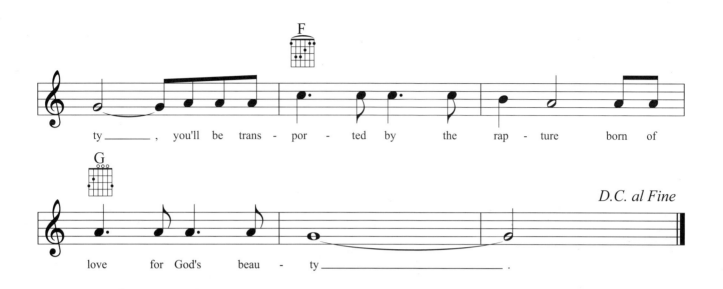

ty _____ , you'll be trans - por - ted by the rap - ture born of

D.C. al Fine

love for God's beau - ty _____ .

Friendship

Text: 'Abdu'l-Bahá
Music: Tim Urbonya, 2001

If you de - sire ___ with all your heart friend- ship with ev' - ry race on ___ earth, your thought, spi - ri - tual and po - si - tive will spread, will be - come the de - sire, the de - sire of o - thers. Grow - ing stron ___ - ger and stron - ger un -

til it rea - ches the minds, the minds of all men.

De - sire _____ with all your heart

friend - ship with ev' - ry race on earth _ . De - sire _____ with all your

heart friend - ship with ev' - ry race on earth _ .

Garden of God

Text and Music: Marg Raynor, 1981

1. Like flow - ers in a gar - den, we grow to - wards the light. The rain will fall up - on us all to make our co - lours bright. *Chorus:* In the

2. The own - er of this gar - den _____ plan - ted it with care. He knew what eve - ry seed would need be - fore he put it there.

3. Daf - fo - dils and dai - sies _____ ro - ses, tu - lips too! They will grow to make a rain - bow, just like me and ___ you!

gar - den of God, *clap, clap, clap* The gar - den of ___ God,

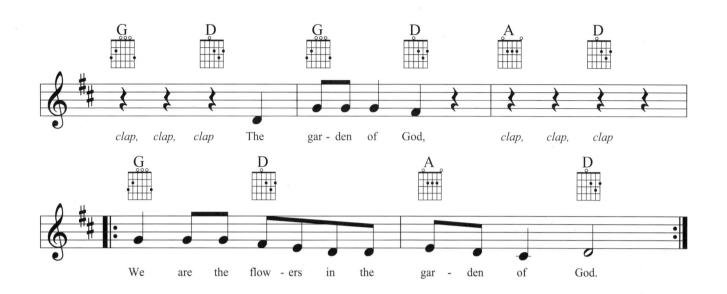

clap, clap, clap The gar - den of God, clap, clap, clap

We are the flow - ers in the gar - den of God.

God is One

Text of 1st verse, and Music: Margaret Jane King, 1962
Text of 2nd verse: ?

1. God is one, man is one, and all the re - li - gions are one _____ .
2. God is love, God is light, and all are as one in His sight _____ .

Land and sea _____ , hill and val - ley, under the beau - ti - ful sun _____ .
Black and white _____ , red and ye - llow, this is the time to u - nite _____ .

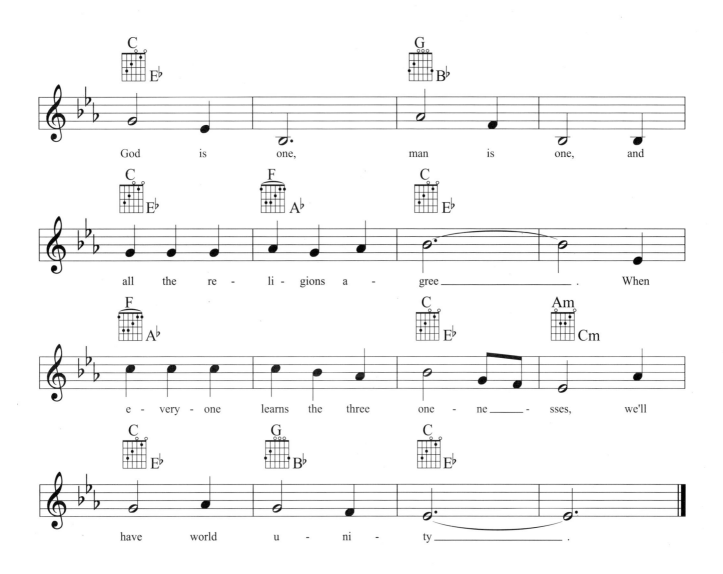

God is one, man is one, and all the re - li - gions a - gree _____. When e - ve-ry - one learns the three one - ne ____ - sses, we'll have world u - ni - ty _____.

God is Sufficient unto Me

The French verse is a paraphrase; the third line is in Haitian Creole, and the origins of both unknown
Le texte en français est une paraphrase. La troisième ligne est en créole haïtien.
Les origines de ces deux textes sont inconnues.
Text: taught by Bahá'u'lláh to the Bábis in the Siyah-Chal
Music/Musique : ?

God is su - ffi - cient un - to me, He ___
Dieu me su - ffit, Il est vrai - ment Ce - lui qui su -
Cé Bon ___ Dyé qui su - fi pour moué, En ___

ve - ri - ly, is the All - Suf - fi ___ - cing.
ffit à tout. Que ce - lui qui est con - fiant,
vé - ri - té Cé li méme ki kap su - fi

In Him let the trus - ting trust ___ .
pla - ce sa con - fiance en lui ___ .
En nous mette con - fiance nan li ___ .

56

Good Neighbours Come in All Colours

Text and Music: Dick Grover, 1968

"inspired by a bumper sticker on the car ahead of me, on the way to Green Acre
Bahá'í School, which said, 'Good neighbours come in all colours' "

Chorus: Good neigh - bours come in all co - lours ___ ,

black, red, yel - low and tan. Our out - sides may look

diff - erent, but we're the fa - mily of wo - man and man.

1. When my door - bell starts to ring, I can't see the
2. When my neigh - bour starts to cry, it hurts her and
3. When my neigh - bours want to share joy and hap - pi - ness

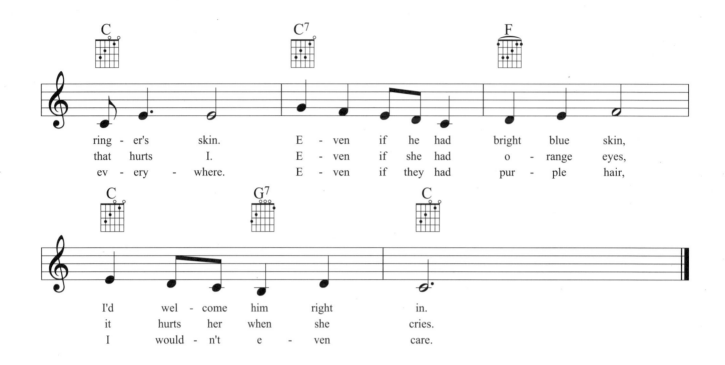

C			C⁷					F		
ring -	er's	skin.	E -	ven	if	he	had	bright	blue	skin,
that	hurts	I.	E -	ven	if	she	had	o -	range	eyes,
ev -	ery -	where.	E -	ven	if	they	had	pur -	ple	hair,

C		G⁷		C
I'd	wel - come	him	right	in.
it	hurts her	when	she	cries.
I	would - n't	e - ven		care.

Harmony (Harmonie)

Text and Music/Paroles et musique : Ariel Barkley, 1986

Har - mo - ny, har - mo - ny, har - mo - ny for
Har - mo - nie, har - mo - nie, har - mo - nie, oui

you and me. Be a friend and you will see, There's
mes a - mis. Vous et moi ___ , dans la vie ___ ,

hap - pi - ness in har - mo - ny!
Le bon - heur, c'est l'har - mo - nie !

59

Head to Toe

Music: Alfred Côté, 1995
Text: ?

Capo 1st fret

I have my eyes, so I can see the

beau - ti - ful world God made 'round me; I have my ears, so I can hear the

sounds of the world and I know He's near; I have my heart, so I can feel God's

love for me and I know He's real; I have my mind, so I can know that

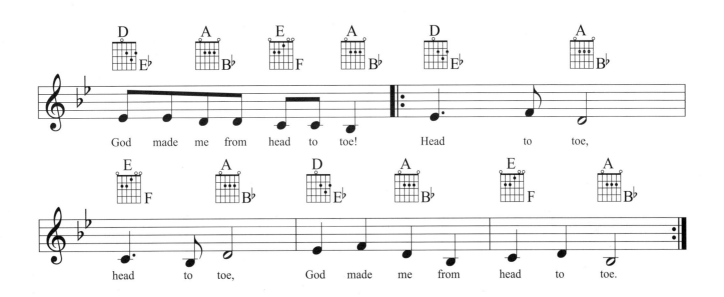

God made me from head to toe! Head to toe,

head to toe, God made me from head to toe.

He Who Puts His Trust in God

Text: the Báb – to be recited 19 times
Music: Anis Mangenda, 2001
*This song is sung as an echo. See contrasting note heads;
use a simple drum beat with vocals.*

He who puts his trust in God _____ ,
He who puts his trust in

God ____ will suf ____ - fice him _____ . and
God _____ , God ____ will suf ____ - fice

he who fears _____ God _____ ,
him _____ . and he who fears _____

God ____ will send him re - lief _____ .
God _____ , God ____ will send him re -

lief _____ .

Hidden Word No. 1 (Arabic)

Text: Bahá'u'lláh
Music: Ariel Barkley, 1986

O SON OF SPI - RIT! My first coun - cil is this _____ : Pos - sess a pure, kind - ly and ra - di - ant heart, that thine may be _____ a so - ve - reign - ty an - cient, im - pe - rish - a - ble and e - ver - last - ing.

Hidden Word No. 4 (Arabic)

Text: Bahá'u'lláh
Music: Ariel Barkley, 1986

I loved thy cre - a - tion, hence I cre-a-ted thee. Where - fore, do thou love Me, that I may name thy name and fill thy soul with the spi - rit of life.

Hidden Word No. 5 (Arabic)

Text: Bahá'u'lláh
Music: Ruth Vander Stelt, 1998

Love Me, that I may love thee, O thou son of be - ing! If thou lo - vest Me not, My love can in no wise re - ach thee, My love can in no wise reach thee, Know this, O My ser - vant!

Hidden Word No. 22 (Arabic)

Text: Bahá'u'lláh
Music: Ariel Barkley, 1986

No - ble _____ have I cre - a - ted thee,

yet thou hast a - based thy - self. Rise then un - to

that for which thou was cre - a _____ - ted.

Hidden Word No. 36 (Arabic)

May be sung as a round, excluding first "O son of man!".

Text: Bahá'u'lláh
Music: Ruth Vander Stelt, 1998

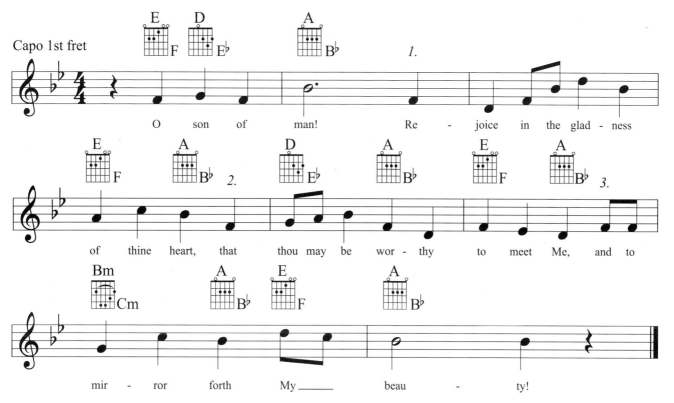

Capo 1st fret

O son of man! Re - joice in the glad - ness of thine heart, that thou may be wor - thy to meet Me, and to mir - ror forth My _____ beau - ty!

Hidden Word No. 55 (Arabic)

Voir aussi le texte en français : la Parole cachée n° 55 en arabe.
Text/Paroles : Bahá'u'lláh
Music and Arrangement/Musique et arrangements : Ruth Vander Stelt, 2000

In this new age the Manifest Light hath, in His holy Tablets, specifically proclaimed that music, sung or played, is spiritual food for soul and heart. The musician's art is among those arts worthy of the highest praise, and it moveth the hearts of all who grieve.

Selections from the writings of 'Abdu'l-Bahá

Hidden Word No. 5 (Persian)

Text: Bahá'u'lláh
Music: Ruth Vander Stelt, 1998

O son, O son of dust! Ve - ri - ly, Ve - ri - ly_____, I say un - to thee: Of_____ all men the most ne - gli - gent is he that dis - pu - teth i - dly and see - keth to ad - vance him - self o'er his bro - ther.

69

Hidden Word No. 81 (Persian)

Text: Bahá'u'lláh
Music: Ruth Vander Stelt, 2000

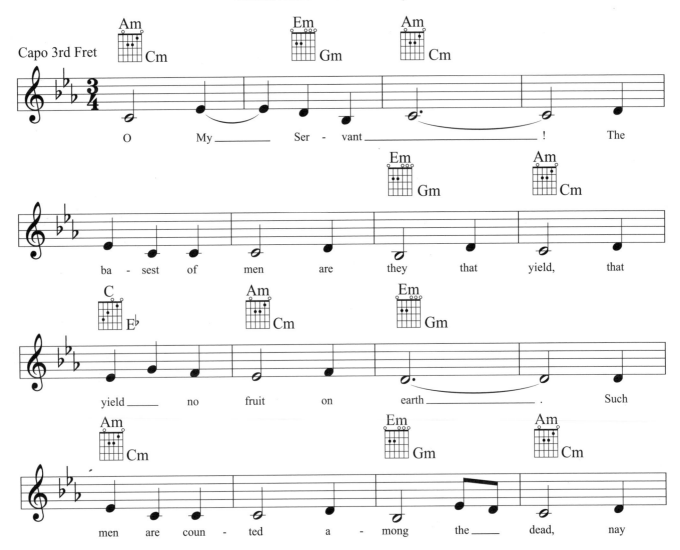

O My ____ Ser - vant _____ ! The
ba - sest of men are they that yield, that
yield ____ no fruit on earth _____ . Such
men are coun - ted a - mong the ____ dead, nay

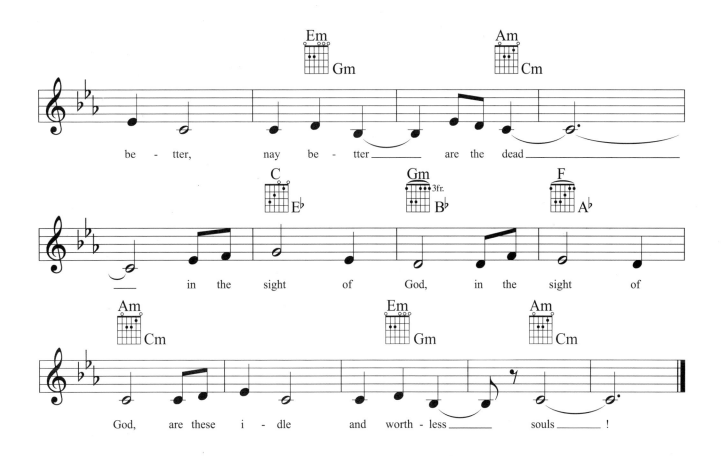

be - ter, nay be - ter _____ are the dead _____

____ in the sight of God, in the sight of

God, are these i - dle and worth - less _____ souls _____ !

Hollow Reed

Text: unauthenticated prayer
Music: Alfred Côté, 1992
The composer suggests that this song be sung a capella.

O ___ God ___ ! Make me a ho- llow reed ___

___ from which the pith of self ___ hath been loaned ___ , that

I ___ may be - come ___ a clear ___ cha ___ - nnel through

which Thy love ___ may flow to o ___ - thers. O ___ God, O ___ God ___ , make

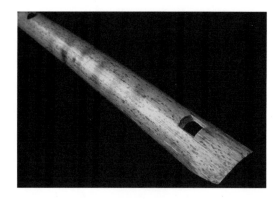

me a ho - llow reed, make of me a ho - llow reed _____ from which the

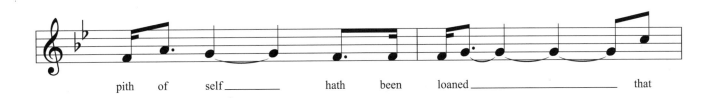

pith of self _____ hath been loaned _____ that

I may be - come, Yá Ba - há _____ a clear cha - nnel, Yá Ba-há-'u'l-Ab - há _ , through

which Thy love _____ may flow to o _____ - thers. O _____

God _____ ! Make me a ho - llow re - ed _____ .

I Think You're Wonderful

Text and Music: Red and Kathy Grammer, 1986

Intro - instrumental

I think you're won - der - ful __ ! When some - bod - y says that to me, I feel won - der - ful __ , as won - der - ful can

be.   It   makes   me   wan - na say _____ the

same thing to some - bod - y new,   And by the way, I've been

3rd Time to Coda

mean - ing to say _____ I think you're won - der - ful   too _____ . 1. When we
                                                                           2. When each

prac - tice this phrase in the most hon - est way   and   find some - thing spec - ial in
one of us feels im __ - por - tant in - side _____ ,   Lo - ving and gi - ving and

some - one each day. We'll   lift up the world one   heart at a time ___ . It
glad we're a - live _____ ,   Oh what a dif - ference we'll make in each day ___ , And

all starts by say - ing this one sim - ple line _____ :
all be - cause some - one de - ci - ded to say _____ :

Coda

too. And by the way, I've been mean - ing to say,

I think you're won - der - ful too.

If an Animal be Sick

Text: 'Abdu'l-Bahá
Music: Tim Urbonya, 2001

If an a - ni - mal be sick, let the chil - dren try to heal it; if it be hun - gry, let them feed it _____ ; if thir - sty _____ , let them quench its ____ thirst ____ ; if wea - ry, let them see that it rests ___

If an a-ni-mal be sick, let the chil-dren try to heal it_____

_____; if it be hun-gry, let them feed it_____; if thir-sty_____; let them

quench its____ thirst__; if wea-ry, let them see that it rests_____, if

wea-ry, let them see that it rests_____.

I Have Found Bahá'u'lláh

Text and Music/Paroles et musique : Miss Nosisana Velem
French paraphrase/Paraphrase en français : Ruth Vander Stelt

1, 2, 3. I have found Ba - há - 'u' - lláh _____ in the
4. Al _____ - láh - 'u' - Ab _____ - há _____ , Al _____ -
5. Hmmm (humming)....
6. J'ai trou - vé Ba - há - 'u' - lláh _____ au _____

ear - ly days of my life. I will keep Him in my
láh _____ - 'u' - Ab - há, Al _____ - láh - 'u' - Ab _____ -
temps de ma _____ jeu - nesse. Dans mon cœur il res - te -

heart _____ and stay with Him for - e - ver.
há _____ and stay with Him for - e - ver.
and stay with Him for - e - ver.
ra _____ , main - te - nant et pour _____ tou - jours.

Inonde du soleil

Text: Bahá'u'lláh and 'Abdu'l-Bahá, in *Bahá'u'lláh et l'Ère Nouvelle*
Paroles: Bahá'u'lláh et 'Abdu'l-Bahá dans Bahá'u'lláh et l'ère nouvelle
Music/Musique: Chantal Daigle, 1993

Bé - ni est ce - lui_____ qui ai - me son frè_____ - re plus que lui - mê_____ - me, plus que lui - mê_____ - me.

Ce - lui - là_____ est du peuple_____ de Ba - há - 'u'l - láh_____ _____ , Ba - há - 'u'l - láh_____ ; Ba - há - 'u'l - láh_____

Pre - nez garde de n'of -fen - ser au - cun coeur ___ !

Pre - nez garde de ne ___ ble - sser au - cune â ___ me !

Pre- nez garde ___ de n'être mal -veil - lant en - vers per - son-

ne ! Pre - nez garde ___ de ne pas être u -

ne cause de dé - ses - poir ___ pour quel - que

Par la puissance et le charme de la musique, l'esprit de l'homme s'élève. Elle règne sur eux et à des conséquences sur l'âme des enfants car leurs coeurs sont purs et les mélodies ont une grande influence sur eux.

Sélections des écrits d'Abdu'l-Bahá

Is There Any Remover of Difficulties?

May be sung as a round as indicated by numbers

Text: Prayer by the Báb
Music: Tom Price, 1976

Is there a — ny Re — mo — ver of dif-fi-cul — ties save God? Say ____: Praised be Go — d! He is God! All are His ser — vants, and all a — bide _____ by His bid - ding!

King of Kings

Sung as a round as numbers indicate
Chanté en canon, comme l'indiquent les nombres
Everyone claps on the rest, which falls at the same time in both groups
Tous tapent des mains pour le reste qui arrive au même moment pour les deux groupes.
Text and Music/Paroles et musique : ?

King of kings and Lord of _____ lords _____ , Glo - ry *Clap* Al -
Roi des rois et Prince de _____ paix _____ , Chan - tons : Al -

láh - 'u'Ab - há! Ba - há _____ 'u' - lláh _____
láh - 'u'Ab - há! Ba - há _____ 'u' - lláh _____

Glo - ry *Clap* Al - láh - 'u'Ab - há!
Chan - tons : Al - láh - 'u'Ab - há!

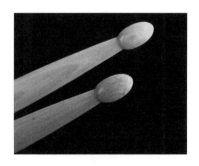

L'administration bahá'íe

Text and Music/Paroles et musique : Ruth Vander Stelt, 2001

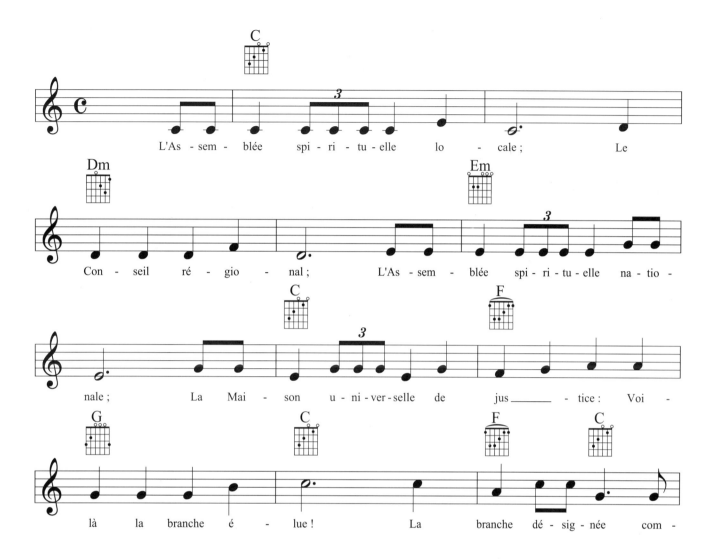

L'As - sem - blée spi - ri - tu - elle lo - cale ; Le Con - seil ré - gio - nal ; L'As - sem - blée spi - ri - tu - elle na - tio - nale ; La Mai - son u - ni - ver - selle de jus _____ - tice : Voi - là la branche é - lue ! La branche dé - sig - née com -

Les talents latents dont ces enfants sont dotés trouveront leur expression par l'intermédiaire de la musique. Pour cette raison, vous devez contribuer à en faire des connaisseurs; enseignez-leur à chanter d'une manière excellente et distinguée.

Sélections des écrits d'Abdu'l-Bahá

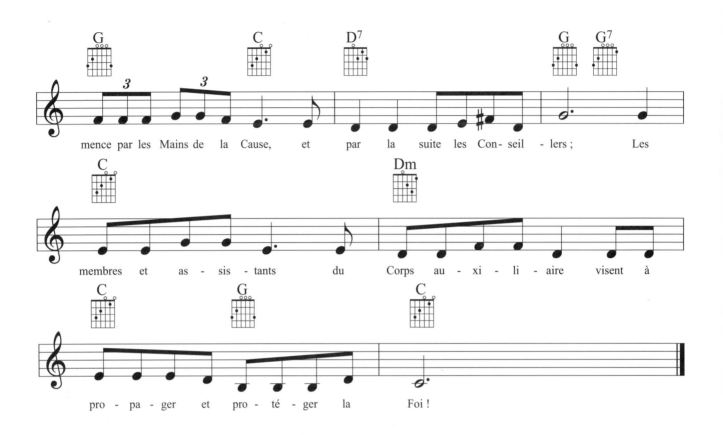

mence par les Mains de la Cause, et par la suite les Con - seil - lers ; Les

membres et as - sis - tants du Corps au - xi - li - aire visent à

pro - pa - ger et pro - té - ger la Foi !

La chanson des prophètes

Text and Music/Paroles et musique : Jack Lenz, Suzanne Hébert, 1986

Refrain : No - é, A - bra - ham, Krish - na ___ , Mo - ïse, Zo - ro - as - tre,

Boud - dha ___ , Jé - sus - Christ, Ma - ho - met _____ , le

Báb et Ba - há - 'u'l - láh láh. 1. Ils sont

les ra - yons ___ d'un même so - leil ___ , Ils sont dif ___ - fé - rents, et ils

---

Chante, ô Mon serviteur, les versets que tu as reçus de Dieu, comme chantent ceux qui furent admis près de Lui, afin que la douceur de ta mélodie embrase ton propre coeur et attire les coeurs de tous les hommes.

Sélections des écrits de Bahá'u'lláh

sont pa - reils___, Comme les é - toiles d'un mê - me ciel___, Comme les

cou - leurs d'un seul arc ___ - en - ciel *Refrain*   2. Com - me les

sai - sons___   qui tou - jours s'en - chaî - nent___   Ils sont ve -

nus jus - qu'à toi___   pour te di - re___ « Je t'ai - me » *Refrain*

Jé - sus - Christ, Ma - ho - met_____ , le Báb et Ba - há - 'u' - lláh.

La courte prière de guérison

Text/Parole : Bahá'u'lláh
Music/Musique : Ruth Vander Stelt, 2000

Ton nom est ma gué - ri - son, ô mon Dieu, et ton

sou - ve - nir est mon re - mè - de. Ê - tre près de toi est mon es -

poir _____ , et mon a - mour pour toi est mon com - pa - gnon, Ta mi -

sé - ri - corde est ma gué - ri - son et mon sou - tien en ce monde

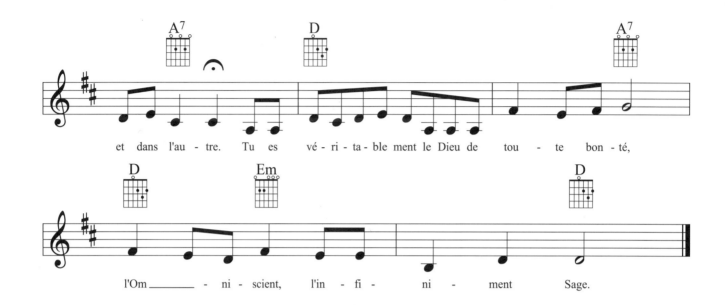

et dans l'au - tre. Tu es vé - ri - ta - ble ment le Dieu de tou - te bon - té,

l'Om _____ - ni - scient, l'in - fi - ni - ment Sage.

La grande prière de guérison

La première portion chantée est indiquée en gras ;
les portions subséquentes à chanter sont indiquées par : ---
Voir texte complet de la prière à la page 92

Toi qui suf - fis à tout, Toi qui___ gué___ ris,

Toi l'É - ter - nel___, Ô Sei - gneur é - ter - nel!

La grande prière de guérison

La première portion chantée est indiquée en gras ;
les portions subséquentes à chanter sont indiquées par : ---

Il est Celui qui guérit, Celui qui suffit à tout, Celui qui assiste, Celui qui toujours pardonne, le Très-Miséricordieux.

Je t'invoque, ô toi l'Exalté, toi le Fidèle, toi le Glorieux !
Toi qui suffis à tout, toi qui guéris, toi l'Éternel, ô Seigneur éternel !
Je t'invoque, ô toi le Souverain, toi qui exaltes, toi le Juge !---

Je t'invoque, ô toi l'Incomparable, toi l'Intemporel, toi l'Unique !---

Je t'invoque, ô toi le Très-Loué, toi le Sanctifié, toi qui secours !---

Je t'invoque, ô toi l'Omniscient, toi le Très-Sage, toi le Très-Grand !---

Je t'invoque, ô toi le Clément, toi le Majestueux, toi qui ordonnes !---

Je t'invoque, ô toi le Bien-Aimé, toi l'Adoré, toi l'Extasié !---

Je t'invoque, ô toi le Très-Fort, toi qui soutiens, toi le Puissant !---

Je t'invoque, ô toi le Dominateur, toi qui subsistes par toi-même !---

Je t'invoque, ô toi l'Esprit saint, toi la Lumière, toi le Plus-Manifeste !---

Je t'invoque, ô toi que tous recherchent, toi l'Illustre, toi le Caché !---

Je t'invoque, ô toi l'Imperceptible, toi le Victorieux, toi le Dispensateur !---

Je t'invoque, ô toi le Tout-Puissant, toi qui secours, toi qui tiens secrets les péchés !---

Je t'invoque, ô toi le Créateur, toi qui remplis d'extase, toi le Destructeur !---

Je t'invoque, ô toi qui élèves, toi qui rassembles, toi qui exaltes !---

Je t'invoque, ô toi l'Excellent, toi l'Indépendant, toi le Généreux !---

Je t'invoque, ô toi le Bienfaisant, toi le Patient, toi le Créateur !---

Je t'invoque, ô toi le Très-Sublime, toi le Magnifique, toi le Prodigue !---

Je t'invoque, ô toi le Dieu de justice, toi le Miséricordieux, toi le Pourvoyeur !---

Je t'invoque, ô toi l'Irrésistible, toi l'Intemporel, toi le Très-Sage !---

Je t'invoque, ô toi le Munificent, toi l'Ancien des jours, toi le Magnanime !---

Je t'invoque, ô toi qui es bon envers tous, toi le Compatissant, toi le Très-Bienfaisant !---

Je t'invoque, ô toi le Havre suprême, toi le seul Refuge, toi le Protecteur !---

Je t'invoque, ô toi l'ultime Secours, toi que tous invoquent, toi qui vivifies !---

Je t'invoque, ô toi le Révélateur, toi qui ravis, toi le Très-Clément !---

Je t'invoque, ô toi qui es mon Âme, toi mon Bien-Aimé, toi ma Foi !---

Je t'invoque, ô toi suprême Échanson, toi Seigneur d'absolu, toi l'Inestimable !---

Je t'invoque, ô toi l'ultime Souvenir, le Nom le plus noble, la Voie la plus ancienne !---

Je t'invoque, ô toi le Très-Loué, toi le Très-Saint, toi le Sancitifié !---

Je t'invoque, ô toi le Libérateur, toi le Conseiller, toi l'Émancipateur !---

Je t'invoque, ô toi le Compagnon, toi le Médecin, toi le Charmeur !---

Je t'invoque, ô toi le Glorieux, toi la Beauté, toi le Généreux !---

Je t'invoque, ô toi l'ultime Confident, toi l'Amant suprême, toi le Seigneur de l'aurore !---

Je t'invoque, ô toi qui enflammes, toi qui illumines, toi qui enchantes !---

Je t'invoque, ô toi Seigneur de bonté, toi le

Très-Compatissant, toi le Très-Clément !---
Je t'invoque, ô toi l'Immuable, toi qui con-
fères la vie, toi la Source de toute existence !---
Je t'invoque, ô toi l'Omniprésent, toi dont le
regard embrasse toutes choses, toi le Seigneur
de l'éloquence !---
Je t'invoque, ô toi qui es manifeste bien que
caché, invisible quoique renommé, toi
l'Observateur que tous cherchent !---

Je t'invoque, ô toi qui éprouves les amants,
toi qui es clément envers les méchants !---
Ô toi qui suffis à tous, je t'invoque, ô toi qui
suffis à tout ! Ô toi qui guéris, je t'invoque, ô
toi qui guéris ! Ô toi qui subsistes, je t'invoque, ô toi qui subsistes ! toi l'Éternel, ô
Seigneur éternel!

Sanctifié es-tu, ô mon Dieu ! Je t'implore, par ta générosité qui fit s'ouvrir toutes grandes les
portes de ta faveur et de ta grâce, par laquelle le temple de ta sainteté fut établi sur le Trône d'é-
ternité et par ta miséricorde par laquelle tu as invité toutes choses créées à la table de tes faveurs
et de tes dons ; et par ta grâce par laquelle tu répondis toi-même par ta parole « Oui » pour tous
ceux qui sont dans les cieux et sur la terre à l'heure où ta souveraineté et ta grandeur furent
révélées, et à l'aube où la puissance de ton empire fut manifestée. Et à nouveau, je t'implore, par
ces noms les plus beaux, par ces attributs les plus sublimes et les plus nobles, et par ton souvenir
le plus exalté, et par ta beauté pure et immaculée, et par ta lumière scellée dans le Saint-
Sanctuaire, et par ton nom enveloppé du vêtement de l'affliction, chaque matin et chaque soir,
de protéger le porteur de cette tablette bénie et quiconque la récite, et quiconque la rencontre,
et quiconque passe près de la maison dans laquelle elle se trouve ; puis de guérir par elle tous les
malades et les souffrants et les pauvres, de toute adversité et de toute détresse, de toute affliction
intolérable et de tout chagrin et de guider par elle quiconque désire pénétrer dans les sentiers de
ta direction et les chemins de ton pardon et de ta grâce.

Tu es en vérité le Puissant, Celui qui suffit à tout, Celui qui guérit, le Protecteur, le Dispensateur,
le Compatissant, le Très-Généreux, le Très-Miséricordieux.

Let Thy Breeze Refresh Them

Text: 'Abdu'l-Bahá
Music: Laura Rowe, 1999
Arrangement: Jim Styan

Chorus: O my Lord! O my Lord! I am a child of ten-der years.

Nou-rish me from the breast of Thy mer - cy.

1. Train me in the bo-som of Thy lo_____ - ve.

E - du - cate me in the school___ of Thy gui_____ - dance. De -

The latent talents with which the hearts of these children are endowed will find expression through the medium of music. Therefore, you must exert yourselves to make them proficient; teach them to sing with excellence and effect.

The Promulgation of Universal Peace, 'Abdu'l-Bahá

94

ve -lop me un - der the sha - dow of Thy boun _____ - ty.

Thou art the Po - wer - ful, the Migh - ty, ve - ri -

to Chorus

ly. 2. De - li - ver me from dark - ness, make me a bril - liant light.

Crown my head with the di - a - dem of e - ter - nal life. Con -

fer up - on me the dis - po - si - tion and na - ture of ___ the right - eous ___

___ .

Free me from ___ un - hap - pi - ness ___

___ . *instrumental*   to Chorus   3. Make me a cause of boun - ty to the

hu - man world.   Suf - fer me to be-come a ser - vant of Thy   thre ___ - shold.

Make   me   a   flo - wer   of   the   rose   gar ___ - den ___

___ . Thou art the Se - er, the Hea - rer, ve - ri - ly ___ .

Look at Me, Follow Me

Text and Music of Refrain: Jackie Elliott
Text and Music of Verses: Tom Price

Capo 1st Fret

1. Be - hold ___ the can - dle, how it gives it light. It
2. You are ___ the an - gels, if your feet be firm. Be

weeps its ___ life a - way ___ , drop by drop ___ , to give its flame ___
stead - fast ___ as a rock ___ , that no earth ___ - ly storm can move ___

___ . You must die to the world and so be born a -
___ . And as you have ___ faith, so shall your po - wers

gain, and en - ter to the king ___ - dom of hea -
be, and know that 'til the end, I'm al - ways with

ut - most po - ver - ty _____ and cry out "Ya Ba - há",

God wi - lling you may do this for me.

1. Teach the Cause, Fo - llow Me, be as I am
2. Serve man - kind, Fo - llow Me, be as I am

'Ab - du'l - Ba - há, 'Ab - du'l - Ba - há.
'Ab - du'l - Ba - há, 'Ab - du'l - Ba - há.

Look at Me, Fo - llow Me, be as I am

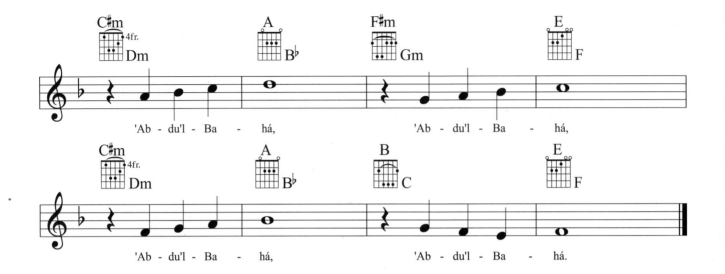

'Ab - du'l - Ba — há,   *'Ab - du'l - Ba — há,*

'Ab - du'l - Ba — há,   *'Ab - du'l - Ba — há.*

French Words for Refrain:
Paroles en français:

Regarde-moi, suis ma voie,
Sois comme je suis,
'Abdu'l-Bahá, 'Abdu'l-Bahá

    2. Aime le monde ...
    3. Enseigne la Cause ...
    4. Sers la Cause ...
    5. Regarde-moi ...

Mon nom à moi

Text/Paroles : ʻAbduʼl-Bahá
Music and Arrangement/Musique et arrangments : Patrick Arnaud, 1998
in order: sung portion, first reading, sung portion, second reading,
sung portion from 3
Dans l'ordre : partie chantée, première lecture, partie chantée, seconde lecture,
partie chantée à partir de 3

Mon ___ nom à ___ moi est ʼAb-duʼl-Ba-há, ma qua-li-fi-ca-tion est ʼAb-duʼl-Ba-há, ma ré-a-li-té est ʼAb-duʼl-Ba-há, ma lou-ange est ʼAb-duʼl-Ba-há ; je n'ai point de ___ nom, de ti-tre, de men-tion, de qua-li-té ___ autres quʼAbduʼl-Ba-há, ma

3

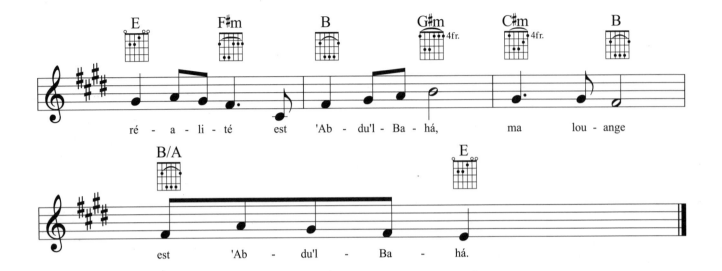

ré - a - li - té est 'Ab - du'l - Ba - há, ma lou - ange

est 'Ab - du'l - Ba - há.

Readings/Lectures :

1. Ma soumission à la Perfection bénie est mon glorieux et resplendissant diadème, et servir l'humanité entière est ma perpétuelle religion.

2. C'est là l'objet de la plus profonde aspiration de mon âme. C'est en cela qu'est ma vie éternelle. C'est de cela qu'est faite ma gloire sans fin.

Morning Prayer

Text: Bahá'u'lláh
Music: Jack Lenz, 1982

I have wa - kened in Thy shel - ter, O my God _____, and it be - com - eth him that seek - eth that shel - ter to a - bide _____ with - in the sanc - tu - a - ry ____ of Thy pro - tec - tion ____ and the strong - hold of Thy de - fense _____ . Il

O Be Joyful!

Sung as a three-part round
Text and Music: ?
Arrangement: Ruth Vander Stelt, 2000

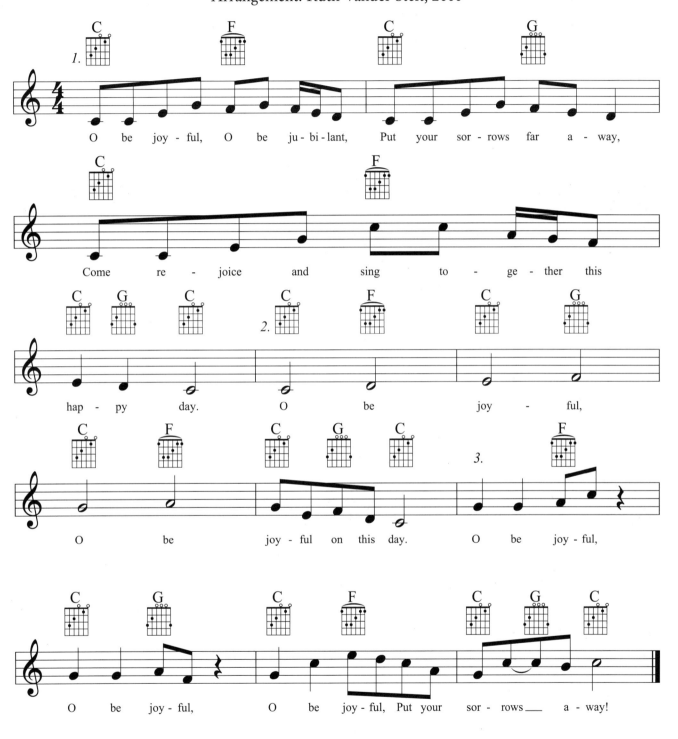

Ô Dieu ! Guide-moi

Text/Paroles : 'Abdu'l-Bahá
Music/Musique : Suzanne Hébert, 1986

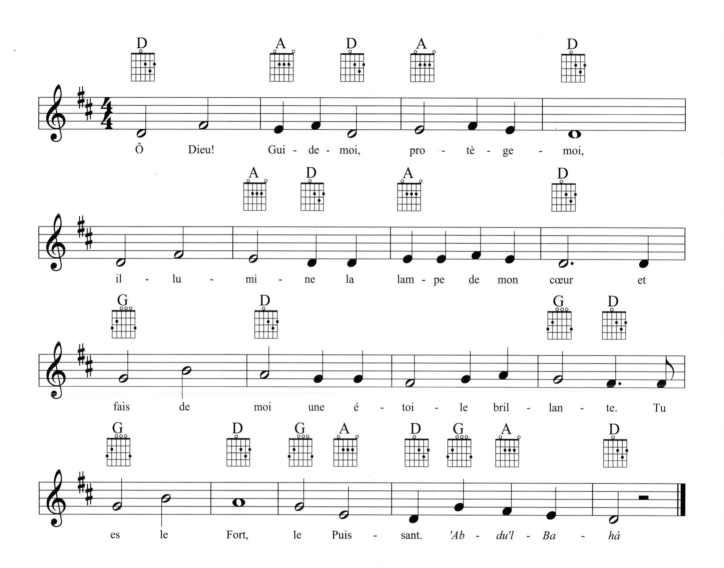

Ô Dieu, pare ma tête

Text/Paroles : Bahá'u'lláh
Music: sung to the tune of Greensleeves, composer unknown
Musique : sur l'air de « *Greensleeves,* » compositeur inconnu
Arrangements : Julie Goudreau

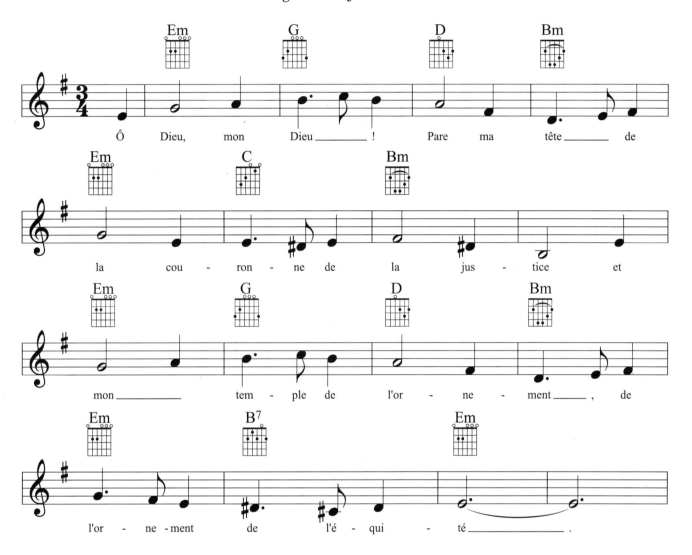

Tu es _____ en vé – ri – té _____ le Pos – ses –
seur _____ de tous les dons et _____ de
tou _____ – tes _____ , de toutes les gé – né – ro – si –
tés _____ , et de toutes les gé – né – ro – si –
tés _____ .

O Dios Guia Me

Spanish version of "O God, Guide Me"
Text: 'Abdu'l-Bahá
Music: ?

O Dios gui - a me, O Dios pro - te - ge me,

I - llu - min - a la lam - pa - ra de mi co - ra - zon

y hace de mi un - a e - stre - lla bril - lant - e. Tu e - res el fuer - te

y el po - de - ro - so, Tu e - res el fuer - te y el po - de - ro - so.

English Pronunciation Key:

the Spanish "r" is rolled on the tip of the tongue

O Dee-oh-s gee-a may
O Dee-oh-s pro-tay-hay may
Ee-lou-mee-na la lam-pa-ra duh mee koh-ra-ssone
ee hass day mee ou-na es-tray-a bree-ant-ay.
Tou er-ess el fou-er-tay ee el po-day-ro-so (x2)

109

O God Educate These Children

Text: 'Abdu'l-Bahá
Music: Danny Deardorff, 1975

Capo 1st Fret

O God! E - du - cate these chil - dren ___ . These

chil - dren are the plants ___ of Thine or - chard ___ , the flo - wers of Thy

mea - dow ___ , the ro - ses of Thy gar - den. Let Thy rain fall u -

pon them; let the Sun of Re - a - li - ty ___ shine up -

Lift up your voices and sing out the songs of the Abhá Realm. Quench ye the fires of war, lift high the banners of peace, work for the oneness of humankind and remember that religion is the channel of love unto all peoples.

Selections from the writings of 'Abdu'l-Bahá

O God, Guide Me

Text: 'Abdu'l-Bahá
Music: Jack Lenz, 1982

Capo 1st Fret

O God, guide me, pro-tect me, Il-lu-mine the lamp of my hea — rt, and make me a bri-lliant star. Thou art the Migh-ty and Po-wer-ful _____ .

Ô mon Seigneur

Text/Paroles : 'Abdu'l-Bahá
Music: traditional middle-Eastern melody
Musique: Mélodie traditionnelle du Moyen-Orient
Arangement: Josée Cardinal, 2000

Capo 3e touche
Capo 3rd Fret

Lyrics under the staves:

Ô _____ mon Sei - gneur ! ô mon _____ Sei _____ - gneur ! Je suis un

en - fant d'â - ge tendre. Nour - ris - moi du lait de ta mi - sé - ri -

corde. É - lè - ve - moi dans _____ ton a - mour, ins - truis - moi à

l'é - cole de ta di - rec - tion et fais que je gran - disse à l'om - bre de ta bon -

té.   Dé - li - vre - moi   des ___ té _____ nè - bres,   pré - ser - ve -

moi   du ___ mal ___ heur,   fais de moi une   bril - lan - te   lu - mi -

ère,   une   fleur ___ de   ta   ro - se - raie ;   souf - fre   que   je

de - vienne   le   ser - vi - teur   de   ton   sanc - tu -

aire   et   don - ne - moi   les   ap - ti   tudes   et   la   na - ture   des

Endeavor your utmost to compose beautiful poems to be chanted with heavenly music; thus may their beauty affect the minds and impress the hearts of those who listen.

Tablets of 'Abdu'l-Bahá

Parole cachée n° 5 en arabe

Text/Paroles : Bahá'u'lláh
Music/Musique : Chantal Daigle, 1993

Ô fils de l'e - xis - tence ! Ô fils de l'e - xis - tence !

Ai - me - moi pour que je puisse ____ t'ai - mer,

Ai - me - moi pour que je puisse ____ t'ai - mer.

Si tu ne m'aimes pas,

Parole Cachée N° 55 en arabe

Text/Paroles : Bahá'u'lláh
Music/Musique : Ruth Vander Stelt, 2000

Peace is Calling

Text and Music: Ariel Barkley, 1986

Chorus: Call - ing, call - ing, Peace ___ is call - ing, Come an - swer my

friends ___ . Call - ing, call - ing, Peace ___ is call - ing,

Come an - swer my friends ___ .

1. Let's turn our
2. Speak ___ to
3. Work ___ with

1. thoughts and plans to longed - for u ___ ni - ty ___ , and
2. all man - kind of truth to set ___ us free ___ , with
3. ra - diant hearts to speed the Gol ___ - den Day ___ , Peace

1. join our hearts in gen - tle har ___ mo - ny ___ .
2. ser - vice, jus - tice, love, e - qua ___ li - ty ___ .
3. in all the world will come and e - ver stay ___ .

Prayer for the Dead

Text: Bahá'u'lláh
Music: Ruth Vander Stelt, 2002

The Prayer for the Dead is to be used for Bahá'ís over the age of 15. "It is the only Bahá'í obligatory prayer which is to be recited in congregation; it is to be recited by one believer while all present stand."

- the Kitáb-i-Aqdas

(If the dead be a woman, let him say: This is Thy hand-maiden and the daughter of Thy handmaiden, etc...)

O my God! This is Thy servant and the son of Thy servant who hath believed in Thee and in Thy signs, and set his face towards Thee, wholly detached from all except Thee. Thou art, verily, of those who show mercy the most merciful.

Deal with him, O Thou Who forgivest the sins of men and concealest their faults, as beseemeth the heaven of Thy bounty and the ocean of Thy grace. Grant him admission within the precincts

of Thy transcendent mercy that was before the foundation of earth and heaven. There is no God but Thee, the Ever-Forgiving, the Most Generous.

Let him, then, repeat six times the greeting "Alláh'u'Abhá" and then repeat nineteen times each of the following verses:

We all, verily, worship God... (see musical score)

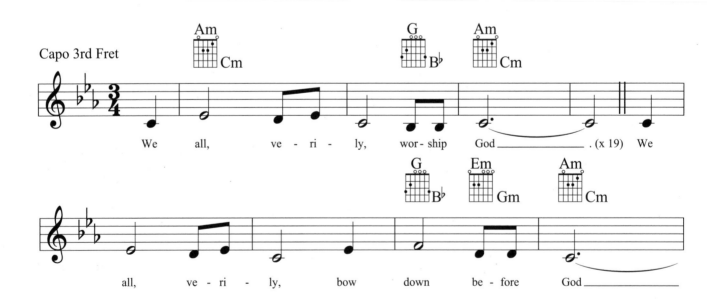

Que ta vie soit pure

Text: Bahá'u'lláh, in "The Advent of Divine Justice"
Paroles : Bahá'u'lláh dans *L'avènement de la justice divine*
Music/Musique : Chantal Daigle, 1994

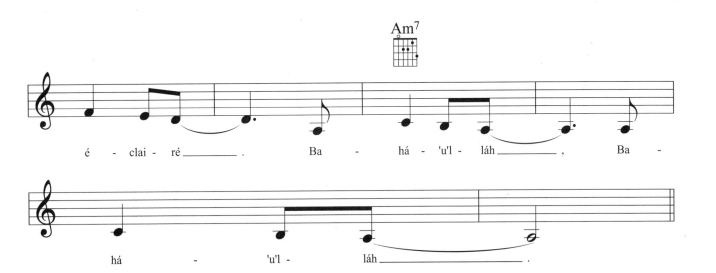

é - clai - ré _____ . Ba - há - 'u'l - láh _____ , Ba -

há - 'u'l - láh _____ .

Que voulez-vous?

Adapted from the traditional Québécois folk song,
"C'est l'aviron qui nous mène en haut"
Adapté du chant folklorique québécois « C'est l'aviron qui nous mène »
(English paraphrase: "Rowing brings us upstream")
Music/Musique : ?
Text/Paroles : Alfred Côté, 1984

1. Que vou - lez - vous? Nous vou - lons l'u - ni - té _____ !
2. Pour - quoi pri - ez - vous? Nous pri - ons pour la paix _____ !
3. Ba - há - 'u' - lláh, c'est la gloi - re du Pè - re,

Mais l'u - ni - té, c'est le dé - sir pro - fond de
Mais oui, la paix, elle se - ra é - ta - blie par
Jé - sus l'a dit, qu'il en - ver - rait sur ter - re

Refrain: Ba - há - 'u' - lláh, qui nous ai - me, qui nous ai - me,

Ba - há - 'u' - lláh, qui nous mène en haut.

Qui hormis Dieu ?

Text/Paroles : the Báb/Le Báb
Music/Musique : Andrea Graham, 1992

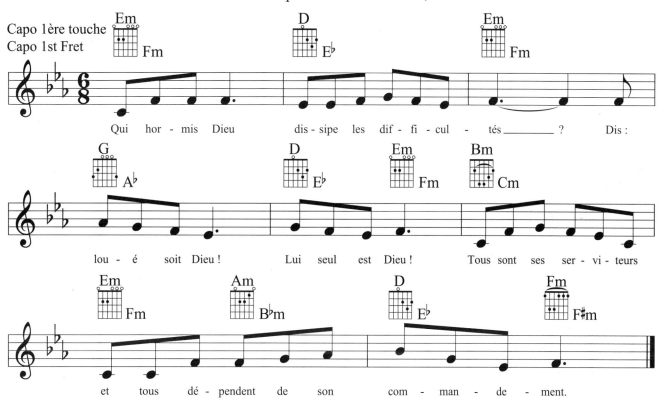

Capo 1ère touche
Capo 1st Fret

Qui hor - mis Dieu dis - sipe les dif - fi - cul - tés _____ ? Dis :

lou - é soit Dieu ! Lui seul est Dieu ! Tous sont ses ser - vi - teurs

et tous dé - pendent de son com - man - de - ment.

Radiant Star

Text: 'Abdu'l-Bahá
Music: Tim Urbonya, 2001

God has crowned you with ho - nor ____ and in your heart has He set a ra - di ____ - ant, ra - diant star. Ve - ri - ly the light there - of shall brigh - ten the whole _____ world _____ .

Ra - di - ant star, Ra - di - ant

star, ve - ri - ly the light there - of shall brigh - ten the whole _____

world _____ .

Say: God Sufficeth

See also French version "Dis : Dieu suffit à tout"
May be sung as a four part round, as numbers indicate
Text: the Báb
Music: Tom Price, 1972

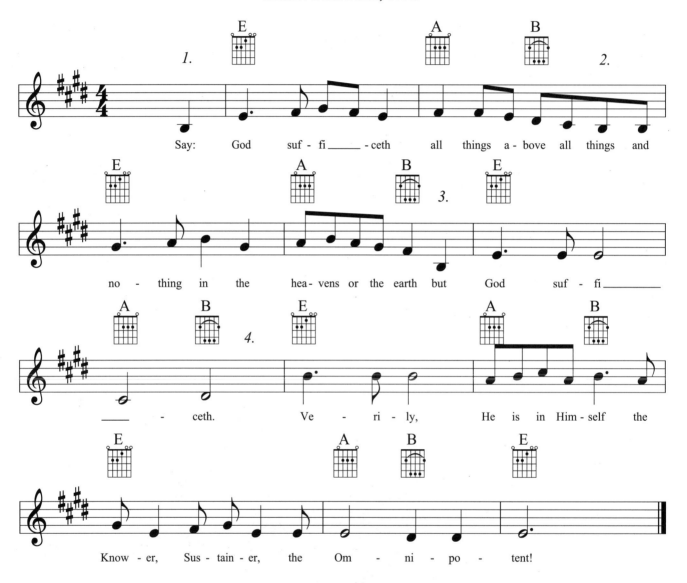

Say: God suf - fi ____ -ceth all things a - bove all things and no - thing in the hea - vens or the earth but God suf - fi _____ ____ -ceth. Ve - ri - ly, He is in Him - self the Know - er, Sus - tain - er, the Om - ni - po - tent!

See the World as One

Text and Music: Ariel Barkley, 1998

1. We are chil - dren with a great un - fold - ing des - ti -
2. Chil - dren all the world a - round will live in har - mo -
3. Fa - mi - lies will learn to live in love and u - ni -

ny; No - ble be - ings each of us, a
ny, Have the things to live and grow and
ty. Hearts and souls will rise with joy; cre -

new hu - ma - ni - ty. *Chorus:* Come and see the
feel se - cu - ri - ty.
a - tion's dig - ni - ty.

world as one. Home is all this earth. God cre - a - ted

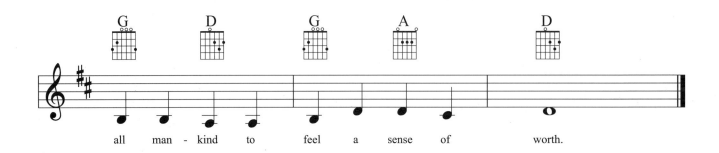

all man - kind to feel a sense of worth.

Shine Your Light on Me, Bahá'u'lláh

Text and Music: Bahá'ís of the South Pacific and Malaysia, approx. 1972
French translation : Dominique Marchal, 2003

1. Shine your light on me, Ba - há'u' - lláh _____, I am o - ver
2. Help me be a lamp, Ba - há'u' - lláh _____, I am o - ver
3. Help me light the world, Ba - há'u' - lláh _____, I am o - ver
4. Help me teach Thy Cause, Ba - há'u' - lláh _____, I am o - ver
5. Shine your light on me, Ba - há'u' - lláh _____, I am o - ver

here, Ba - há'u' - lláh _____, Shine your light on me, Ba - há'u' - lláh __
here, Ba - há'u' - lláh _____, Help me be a lamp, Ba - há'u' - lláh __
here, Ba - há'u' - lláh _____, Help me light the world, Ba - há'u' - lláh __
here, Ba - há'u' - lláh _____, Help me teach Thy Cause, Ba - há'u' - lláh __
here, Ba - há'u' - lláh _____, Shine your light on me, Ba - há'u' - lláh __

_____, Glo - ri - ay, Glo - ri - ay.
_____, Glo - ri - ay, Glo - ri - ay.
_____, Glo - ri - ay, Glo - ri - ay.
_____, Glo - ri - ay, Glo - ri - ay.
_____, Glo - ri - ay, Glo - ri - ay.

French Words/Paroles en français :

Illumine ma vie, Bahá'u'lláh
Je suis toujours là, Bahá'u'lláh
Illumine ma vie, Bahá'u'lláh
«Glorié, glorié»*

2. Fais de moi une lampe ...
3. Que j'éclaire le monde ...
4. Que j'enseigne ta cause ...
5. Illumine ma vie ...

* Cette dernière ligne est une transcription phonétique du texte anglais.

131

Somebody Told Me

based on Bible prophecies
Text and Music: Dick Grover, 1994

Some - bo - dy told me the Lord was a - com - ing and the
time was ve - ry near. Some - bo - dy, some - bo - dy said He was a - com - ing,
some - bo - dy said He was here.

1. Some - bo - dy told me the night would be o - ver and the
2. Some - bo - dy told me the sun would be ri_____ - sing_____
3. Some - bo - dy told me the King - dom was a - com - ing but we

132

C   G⁷

dark - ness would   soon   be   gone.
way   up   high   in   the   air.
di   -   dn't   know   when   or   how.

C   F

Some - bo - dy prayed   for   the   night   to   be   o - ver,
Some - bo - dy prayed   for   the   sun   to   be   ri - sing,
Some - bo - dy prayed   for   the   King - dom   to   get   here---

C   G⁷   C

some - bo - dy said   it   was   dawn.
some - bo - dy said   it   was   there.
some - bo - dy said   it   was   now.

Song of the Months

Text and Music: Jack Lenz and Doug Cameron, 1982

Ba - há, Ja - lál, Ja - mál, 'A - za - mat, Núr, Rah - mat,

Ka - li - mát, Ka - mál, As - má', 'Iz - zat, Mash - íy - yat, 'Ilm,

Qud - rat, Qawl, Ma - sá - il, Sha - raf _ , Sul - tán, Mulk, 'A - lá'.

Splen - dor, Glo - ry and Beau - ty, Gran - deur, Light and Mer - cy,

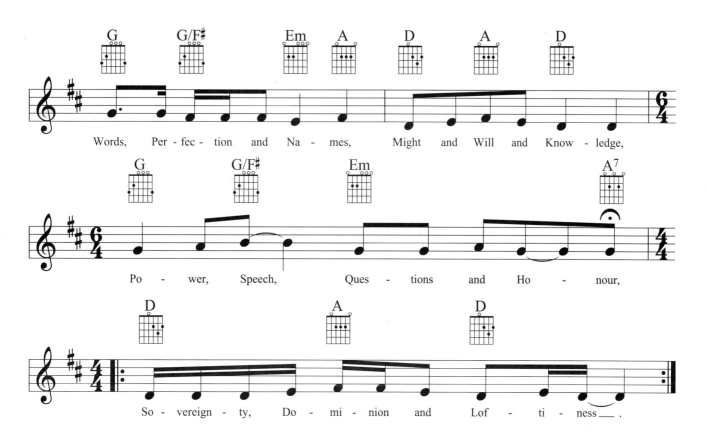

Words, Per - fec - tion and Na - mes, Might and Will and Know - ledge,

Po - wer, Speech, Ques - tions and Ho - nour,

So - vereign - ty, Do - mi - nion and Lof - ti - ness ___ .

BAHÁ
JALÁL
JAMÁL

135

Song of the Prophets

Text and Music: Jack Lenz, 1982

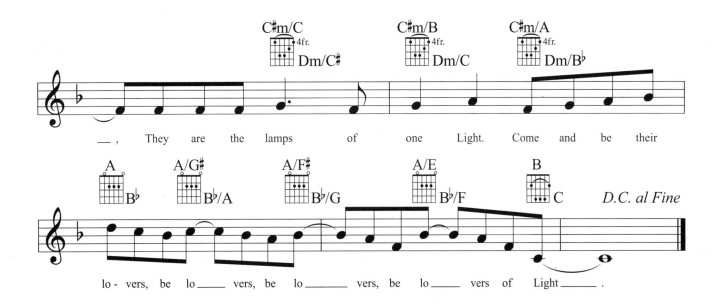

_____, They are the lamps of one Light. Come and be their

lo - vers, be lo ____ vers, be lo ____ vers, be lo ____ vers of Light ____ .

Teaching Peace

Text and music: Red and Kathy Grammer, 1986

Teach - ing peace all the world a - round,
(2nd time, count 1, 2, 3, 4)

You and me, ev - 'ry ci - ty ev - 'ry town, One by one, in our

work and in our play, We are teach - ing peace by what we

do and what we say. (counting ends)

1. It's up to
2. 3. (So take my)

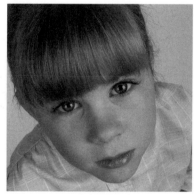

We are teach - ing peace in what we do and what we say. 2. So take my

do and what we say. We are teach - ing peace by what we

D.C. al Fine

do and what we say. do and what we say,

Fine

We are teach - ing peace by what we do and what we say.

The Backbiting Song

Text: Mimi McClellan, Susan Engle
Music: Mimi McClellan, 1973

Jazzy
Not too fast

Intro...

Refrain: When you feel a back-bite co - ming on, Bite it back! Hold it in! Get your-self under con - trol! 'Cause a back - bite can quench the light of the heart and ex - tin - guish the life of the soul.

Therefore ... set to music the verses and the divine words so that they may be sung with soul-stirring melody in the Assemblies and gatherings, and that the hearts of the listeners may become tumultuous and rise towards the Kingdom of Abhá in supplication and prayer.

'Abdu'l-Bahá, Bahá'í World Faith

1. O if you see ___ lit - tle E - mi - ly ___; She has
2. O if you play ___ dur - ing gym to - day ___, And you're
3. O if you spy ___ on your new friend Cy ___, Have

rag - ged clothes; her shoes have ho - ley soles ___, Do you call her
ma - king fun of the way I run ___, Just be - cause I'm
more to eat than a kid twice his size ___, Do you call him

ug - ly ___? Care - ful what you say ___, if you
clum - sy ___,
fat - so ___?

want to feel o - kay when you look back on your day!

The Glory of God

Text and Music: Dick Grover, 1994

1. May the Glo - ry of God shine on you, May the
2. Be a Gate for the Glo - ry to shine through, Be a
3. Serve the Glo - ry in eve - ry thing you do, Serve the
4. May the Glo - ry of God shine on you, May the

Glo - ry of God shine on me and my bro - ther too. As you
Gate for the Glo - ry for me and my sis - ter too. As you
Glo - ry with me and ___ with ___ my fam - ily too. As you
Glo - ry of God shine on you and your neigh - bour too. As you

walk through - out the land, take your bro - ther by the hand, May the
walk through - out the land, take your sis - ter by the hand, Be a
walk through - out the land, take your fam - ily by the hand, Serve the
walk through - out the land, take your neigh - bour by the hand, May the

Glo - ry of God shine on you.
Gate for the Glo - ry to shine through.
Glo - ry in eve - ry thing you do.
Glo - ry of God shine on you.

The Long Healing Prayer

The repetitive portion of the prayer is sung in unison
or in simple harmony (see Appendix);
the rest is read by one or more people.
Text: Prayer by Bahá'u'lláh
Music: Ruth Vander Stelt, 1999

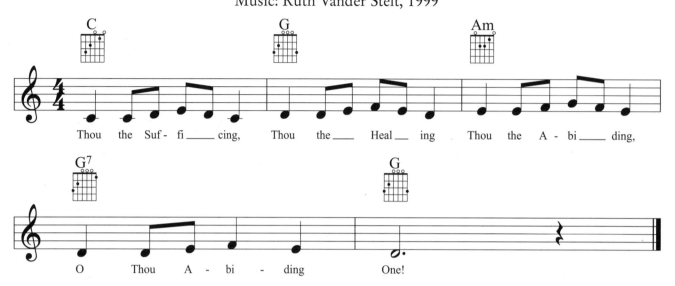

Thou the Suf - fi _____ cing, Thou the _____ Heal _____ ing Thou the A - bi _____ ding,

O Thou A - bi - ding One!

The Long Healing Prayer

The first sung portion is indicated in bold;
Following sung portions are identical to the first and are indicated by : ---

He is the Healer, the Sufficer the Helper, the All-Forgiving, the All-Merciful.

I call on Thee O Exalted One, O Faithful One, O Glorious One!
Thou the Sufficing, Thou the Healing, Thou the Abiding, O Thou Abiding One!
I call on Thee O Sovereign, O Upraiser, O Judge! ---

I call on Thee O Peerless One, O Eternal One, O Single One! ---
I call on Thee O Most Praised One, O Holy One, O Helping One! ---
I call on Thee O Omniscient, O Most Wise, O Most Great One! ---
I call on Thee O Clement One, O Majestic One, O Ordaining One! ---
I call on Thee O Beloved One, O Cherished One, O Enraptured One! ---
I call on Thee O Mightiest One, O Sustaining One, O Potent One! ---
I call on Thee O Ruling One, O Self-Subsisting, O All-Knowing One! ---
I call on Thee O Spirit, O Light, O Most Manifest One! ---
I call on Thee O Thou Frequented by all, O Thou Known to all, O Thou Hidden from all! ---
I call on Thee O Concealed One, O Triumphant One, O Bestowing One! ---
I call on Thee O Almighty, O Succoring One, O Concealing One! ---
I call on Thee O Fashioner, O Satisfier, O Uprooter! ---
I call on Thee O Rising One, O Gathering One, O Exalting One! ---
I call on Thee O Perfecting One, O Unfettered One, O Bountiful One! ---
I call on Thee O Beneficent One, O Withholding One, O Creating One! ---
I call on Thee O Most Sublime One, O Beauteous One, O Bounteous One! ---
I call on Thee O Just One, O Gracious One, O Generous One! ---
I call on Thee O All-Compelling, O Ever-Abiding, O Most Knowing One! ---
I call on Thee O Magnificent One, O Ancient of Days, O Magnanimous One! ---
I call on Thee O Well-guarded One, O Lord of Joy, O Desired One! ---
I call on Thee O Thou Kind to all, O Thou Compassionate with all, O Most Benevolent One! ---
I call on thee O Haven for all, O Shelter to all, O All-Preserving One! ---
I call on Thee O Thou Succorer of all, O Thou Invoked by all, O Quickening One! ---
I call on Thee O Unfolder, O Ravager, O Most Clement One! ---
I call on Thee O Thou my Soul, O Thou my Beloved, O Thou my Faith! ---
I call on Thee O Quencher of thirsts, O Transcendent Lord, O Most Precious One! ---
I call on Thee O Greatest Remembrance, O Noblest Name, O Most Ancient Way! ---
I call on Thee O Most Lauded, O Most Holy, O Sanctified One! ---
I call on Thee O Unfastener, O Counselor, O Deliverer! ---
I call on Thee O Friend, O Physician, O Captivating One! ---
I call on Thee O Glory, O Beauty, O Bountiful One! ---
I call on Thee O the Most Trusted, O the Best Lover, O Lord of the Dawn! ---
I call on Thee O Enkindler, O Brightener, O Bringer of Delight! ---

I call on Thee O Lord of Bounty, O Most Compassionate, O Most Merciful One! ---
I call on Thee O Constant One, O Life-giving One, O Source of all Being! ---
I call on Thee O ThouWho penetratest all thing, O All-Seeing God, O Lord of Utterance! ---
I call on Thee O Manifest yet Hidden, O Unseen yet Renowned, O Onlooker sought by all! ---
I call on Thee O Thou Who slayest the Lovers, O God of Grace to the wicked! ---

O Sufficer, I call on Thee, O Sufficer!
O Healer, I call on Thee, O Healer!
O Abider, I call on Thee, O Abider!
Thou the Ever-Abiding, O thou Abiding One!

Sanctified art Thou, O my God! I beseech Thee by Thy generosity, whereby the portals of Thy bounty and grace were opened wide, whereby the Temple of Thy Holiness was established upon the throne of eternity; and by Thy mercy whereby Thou didst invite all created things unto the table of Thy bounties and bestowals; and by Thy grace whereby Thou didst respond, in Thine own Self with Thy word « Yea! » on behalf of all in heaven and earth, at the hour when Thy sovereignty and Thy grandeur stood revealed, at the dawn-time when the might of Thy dominion was made manifest. And again do I beseech Thee, by these most beauteous names, by these most noble and sublime attributes, and by Thy most Exalted Remembrance, and by Thy pure and spotless Beauty, and by Thy hidden Light in the most hidden pavilion, and by Thy Name, cloaked with the garment of affliction every morn and eve, to protect the bearer of this blessed Tablet, and whoso reciteth it, and whoso cometh upon it, and whoso passeth around the house wherein it is. Heal Thou, then, by it every sick, diseased and poor one, from every tribulation and distress, from every loathsome affliction and sorrow, and guide Thou by it whosoever desireth to enter upon the paths of Thy guidance, and the ways of Thy forgiveness and grace. Thou art verily the Powerful, the All-Sufficing, the Healing, the Protector, the Giving, the Compassionate, the All-Generous, the All-Merciful.

The Pearl

Sung as a round, as numbers indicate
Text: 'Abdu'l-Bahá
Music: Kathryn A. Tahiri

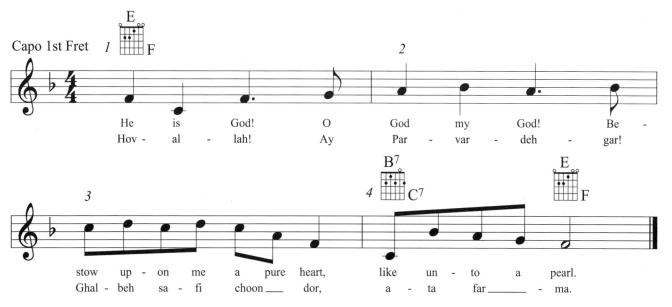

He is God! O God my God! Be-
Hov - al - lah! Ay Par - var - deh - gar!

stow up - on me a pure heart, like un - to a pearl.
Ghal - beh sa - fi choon __ dor, a - ta far _____ - ma.

The Soul is the Sun

Text and Music: Nancy Ward, 1985

Sing verse, then chorus; then divide group in half
and sing both at the same time

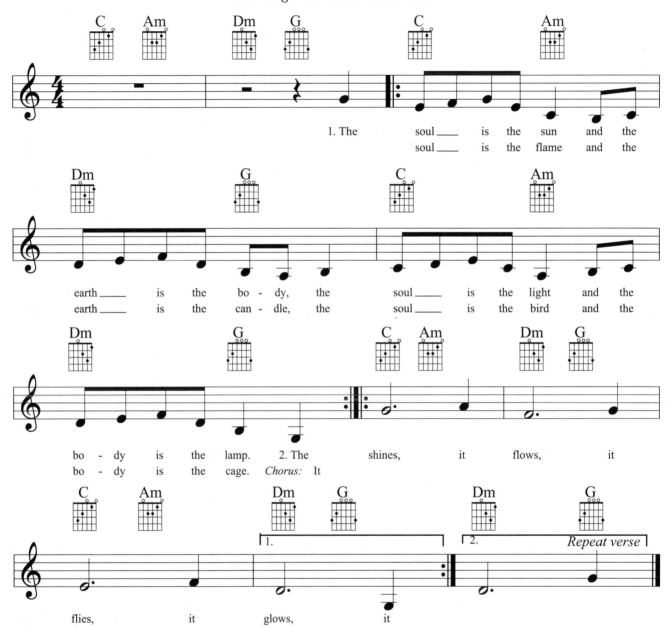

Thokozani

Zulu song from Swaziland
Text and Music: Benjamin Dlamini, 1958
English Text: Russ Garcia; Portugese and French texts: ?
Texte en français : ?
pronounce "th" as "t"

Tho - ko - za - ni ___ ni - na mhla - ba won - ke ___ Le -
Re - joice, re - joice ___ for a new day has dawned, The
Can - tem, can - tem o no - vo dia che - gou ___ o
Ré - jouis - toi, un ___ nou - veau ___ jour a lui _ , ...

li lan - ga lo - ku - kha - nya Tho - ko - za - ni ___ ni - na mhla -
whole wide world is all one fold. Re - joice, re - joice ___ for a new
pla - no de Deus ___ já re - ve - lou. Can - tem, can - tem o no - vo

ba won - ke ___ Le - li lan - ga e - li - khu - lu. O
day has dawned, The plan of God has now been told! The
dia che - gou _ , o pla - no de Deus ___ já re - ve - lou. O

Ku - kho - n'u - kho - lo lu - ka Ba - há ___ Um - hla - mbi wom - hla -
Pro - mised One by the name of Ba - há ___ came to bring a new
pro - me - ti - do de no - me Ba - há ___ Trouxe o No - vo di -

ba
day,
a

Ku - de ku - da - la si - lin - di - le _____ Thi
Let us be hap - py, let _____ us say _____ :
Se - ja - mos fe - li - zes can te mos as - sim _____ :

Yá Ba - há - 'u'l - Ab - há, Thi Yá Ba - há - 'u'l - Ab - há, Thi
Yá Ba - há - 'u'l - Ab - há, Say Yá Ba - há - 'u'l - Ab - há, Say
Yá Ba - há - 'u'l - Ab - há, Diz: Yá Ba - há - 'u'l - Ab - há, Diz:

Yá Ba - há - 'u'l - Ab - há.
Yá Ba - há - 'u'l - Ab - há.
Yá Ba - há - 'u'l - Ab - há.

Words in French:

1. Réjouis-toi, un nouveau jour a lui
   À l'horizon de l'unité
   Prédit par les Messagers du passé
   Bahá'u'lláh est arrivé

Refrain:

   Le messager de Dieu est apparu
   Clamant un nouveau jour
   Soyons heureux et chantons toujours
   Yá Bahá'u'l-Abhá, dis Yá Bahá'u'l-Abhá,
   dis Yá Bahá'u'l-Abhá

2. Krishna, Bouddha, Jésus et Mohammed
   Tous sont de Dieu les messagers
   Au cours des siècles ils nous ont révélé
   Du Créateur la volonté

3. Rejoins la Foi de ceux qui avant toi
   Ont espéré voir l'amitié,
   Un monde uni sans frontières ni conflit
   La religion de l'unité

Thou Seest These Children

Text and Music: Jim Styan, 1999

instrumental

O my God _____ ! Thou see-est these chil - dren _____ who are the twigs _____ of the tree of life _____ . The birds of the meads of sal - va - tion _____ , the pearls of the o-cean of Thy

grace _____ , the ro - ses of the gar - den of Thy gui _____ dance. O

God, our Lord! We sing Thy praise _____ . O God, our Lord! We sing Thy

praise _____ . O my God! We bear wit - ness to Thy

sanc - ti - ty _____ and im - plore fer - vent - ly the hea - ven of Thy

mer - cy _____ to make us lights of gui _____ dance,

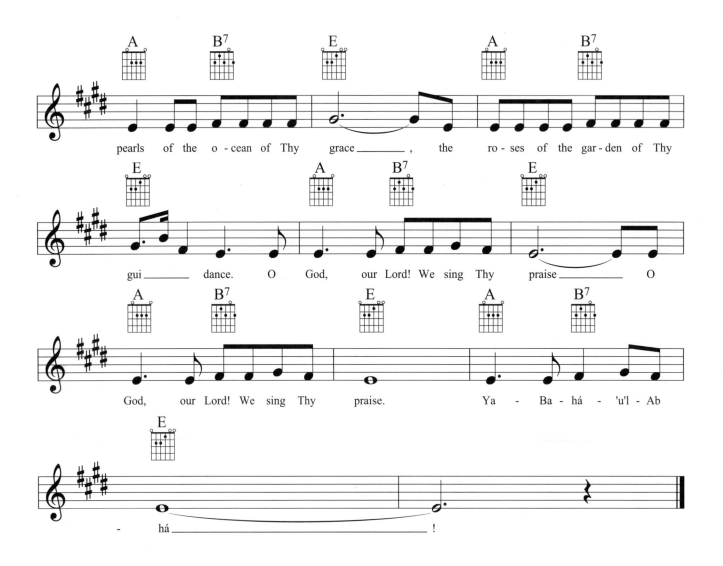

pearls of the o - cean of Thy grace _____, the ro - ses of the gar - den of Thy
gui _____ dance. O God, our Lord! We sing Thy praise _____ O
God, our Lord! We sing Thy praise. Ya - Ba - há - 'u'l - Ab
- há _____ !

Thy Name is My Healing

Text: Bahá'u'lláh
Music and Arrangement: Ruth Vander Stelt, 1998

Thy name is my hea - ling, O God _____ . Re -
mem - brance of Thee is my re ____ - me - dy, O God _____ .
Near - ness to Thee is my hope and love for Thee my com -
pa - nion, O God _____ . Thy mer - cy to me is my

As to the wonderful melody whereby thy spirit was revived, verily it is a melody of the melodies of the divine music, which will cause the spirits to ascend unto the Supreme Horizon and will (cause) the mysteries to be unfolded.

Tablets of 'Abdu'l-Bahá

Tread Ye the Path of Justice

Text: Bahá'u'lláh
Music: Tim Urbonya, 2001
in this call-response song: the leader is indicated in plain text
the responders in italics
bold CAPITAL letters indicate words shouted out
AND ALL TOGETHER ON CAPITAL LETTERS

Tread ye the path of jus_ -tice_ , for this, ve -ri -ly is___ the straight path.

Tread ye the path of jus_ - tice_ , for this ve -ri -ly is___ the **STRAIGHT PATH.**

Tread ye the path, *tread ye the path,* Tread ye the path, *tread ye the path,*

TREAD YE THE PATH OF JUS - TICE_____ , FOR THIS

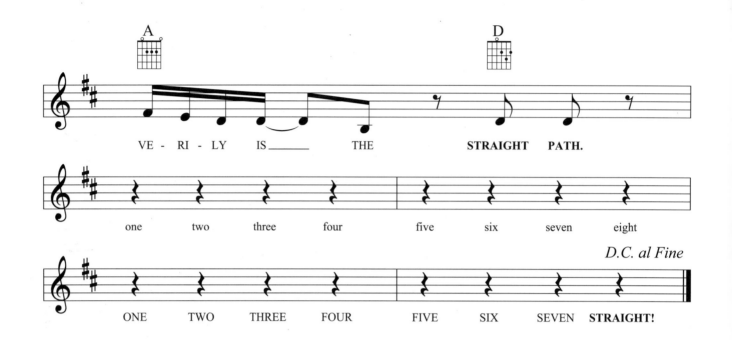

VE - RI - LY IS_____ THE **STRAIGHT PATH.**

one two three four five six seven eight

D.C. al Fine

ONE TWO THREE FOUR FIVE SIX SEVEN **STRAIGHT!**

Virtues Rap

Text and Rythm: John Chesley and Sharon Chesley-Smith, 2001
Sing chorus between each verse
Stomping and clapping continues throughout chorus and verses

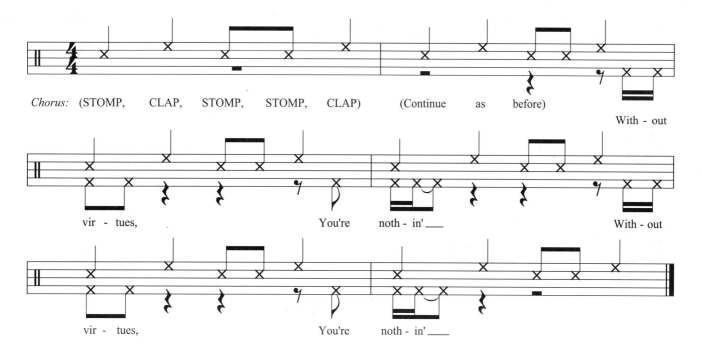

Chorus: (STOMP, CLAP, STOMP, STOMP, CLAP)   (Continue as before)   With - out

vir - tues,   You're noth - in' ___   With - out

vir - tues,   You're noth - in' ___

1. Now follow me closely, it won't take very long.
   Virtues are what bring humanity along.
   We want you to know that we just don't get it,
   Virtues are admired, but rarely get the credit.

2. Now you got your plants and your animals too,
   But they got limits when compared to you.
   It's boys and girls who are gonna win.
   They're the ones who got Virtues within.

3. Now you got your kindness and patience galore.
   Assertiveness and caring are great, that's for sure.
   Courage, love and service and add some forgiveness
   Is what the world wants to see, more of not less.

4. There are lots of virtues, that are really where it's at
   Like cleanliness, respect and that little one, tact.
   And even with our parents, courtesy's a hit.
   The one called enthusiasm's our favorite.

5. We all know about honesty and justice,
   Folks are keen on unity, you'll just have to trust us.
   Determination, detachment, obedience, too--
   With a little dash of reverence, we'll rap them to you.

6. Now all these virtues, you know they're just right
   And that a man with no virtues is a lamp without a light.
   With our virtues revealed, you'll give us the nod.
   Hey, a world full of virtues is a world full of God.

Final Chorus: Without virtues,
You're nothin'.
WITH virtues,
You're SOMETHIN'

We are Bahá'ís

Text and Music: Jack Lenz, 1982

1. To know is to grow _____ , to grow is to
2. Ru - hiy - yih Khá - num _____ , in sor - row and

love _____ , to love is to serve, serve all man -
joy _____ , she loved and she served like 'Ab - du'l - Ba -

kind. *Refrain:* We can be ser - vants of the ser - vants, we can
há.

be lo - vers of the lo - vers; as we grow, we ___ can be the

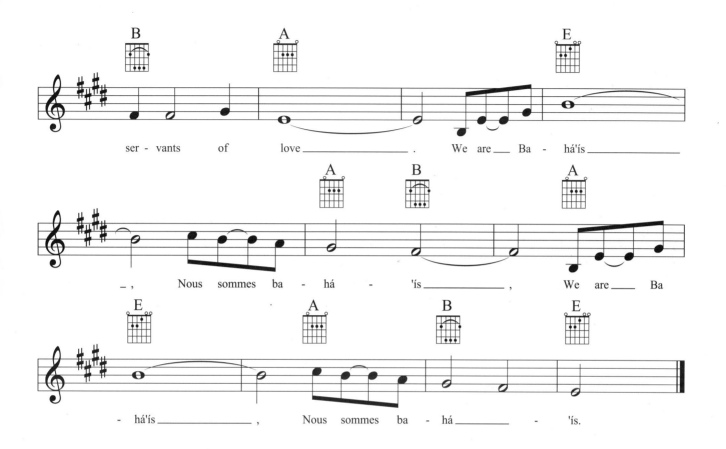

ser - vants of love _____ . We are ___ Ba - há'ís _____

_ , Nous sommes ba - há - 'ís _____ , We are ___ Ba

- há'ís _____ , Nous sommes ba - há _____ - 'ís.

... loose my tongue that it may make mention of Thee and sing Thy praise.

Prayers and Meditations by Bahá'u'lláh

Yá Bahá'u'l-Abhá

Text: Bahá'í appelations
Music: ?
Harmonisation and arrangement: Josée Cardinal, 2000

English paraphrase:

O Thou the Glory of glories,
O Thou the Highest of the high

Yá Hou

Text: Pakistani Bahá'ís, 1980s
Arrangement: Ruth Vander Stelt, 2002
see Arabic pronunciation key

English paraphrase:
O God (x3)
O God of purity
There is no other God but Thee

Paraphrase en français :
Ô Dieu (x3) Ô Dieu de pureté
Il n'y a d'autre Dieu que toi

Appendix One

Full Scores for Selected Songs

Other scores may be obtained from
the various contributors.

Alláh'u'Abhá - 95 times

Sing 5 times to total 95 Alláh'u'Abhás
Text: Incantation ordained in the Most Holy Book, the Kitáb-i-Aqdas
Music: Josée Cardinal, 2000
Arrangement: Ruth Vander Stelt

Hidden Word No. 5 (Arabic)

Text: Bahá'u'lláh
Music: Ruth Vander Stelt, 1998

Love Me, that I may love thee, O thou son of Be - ing! Love Me, that I may love thee, O Thou son of - Be ing! If thou lo - vest Me not, My love can in no wise rea - ch thee

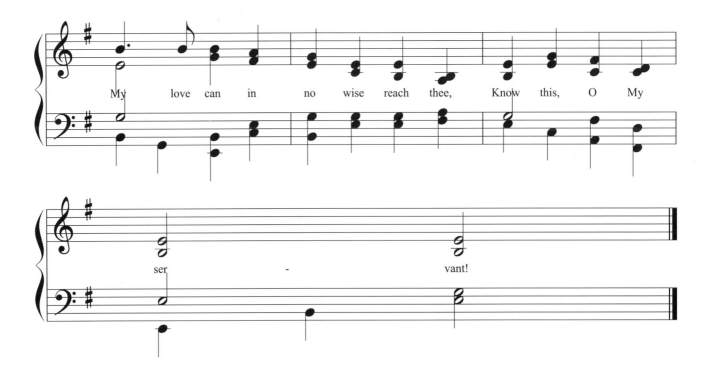

My love can in no wise reach thee, Know this, O My

ser - vant!

Hidden Word No. 36 (Arabic)

May be sung as a round, excluding first "O son of man!"
Text: Bahá'u'lláh
Music: Ruth Vander Stelt, 1998

O SON OF MAN! Re - joice in the glad - ness of thine heart, that thou may be wor - thy to meet Me, and to mir - ror forth My ___ beau - ty!

Hidden Word No. 55 (Arabic)

Text: Bahá'u'lláh
Music and Arrangement: Ruth Vander Stelt, 2000

Bu - sy not thy - self, bu - sy not thy - self, bu - sy not thy - self with this world; For with fire We test, for with fire We test, with fire We test the gold; and with gold We test, and with gold We test, with gold We test Our

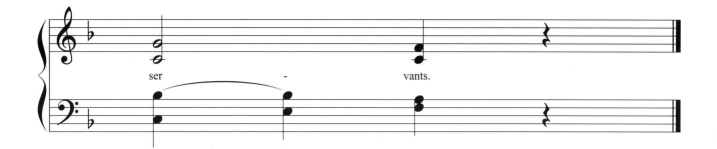

ser - vants.

It is incumbent upon each child to know something of music, for without knowledge of this art the melodies of instrument and voice cannot be rightly enjoyed. Likewise, it is necessary that the schools teach it in order that the souls and hearts of the pupils may become vivified and exhilarated and their lives be brightened with enjoyment.

'Abdu'l-Bahá, The Promulgation of Universal Peace

La courte prière de guérison

Text/Parole : Bahá'u'lláh
Music/Musique : Ruth Vander Stelt, 2000

Ton nom est ma gué-ri-son, Ô mon Dieu, et ton sou-ve-nir est mon re-mè-de. Ê-tre près de toi est mon es-poir_____, et mon a-mour pour toi est mon com-pa-gnon, Ta mi-sé-ri-corde est ma gué-ri-son et mon sou-tien en ce monde

et dans l'au - tre. Tu es vé - ri - ta - ble - ment le Dieu de tou - te bon - té,

l'Om — - ni - scient, l'in - fi - ni - - ment Sage.

La grande prière de guérison

La portion répétée de la prière est chantée ;
le reste est lu par une ou plusieurs personnes.
Voir texte complet de la prière à la page 92
Text/Paroles : Bahá'u'lláh
Music and Arrangement/Musique et arrangements : Ruth Vander Stelt, 1999

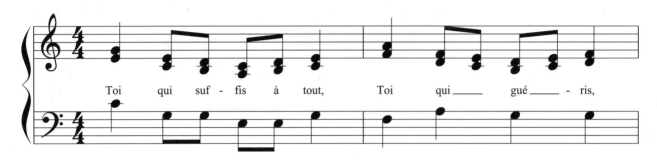

Toi qui suf-fis à tout, Toi qui ___ gué ___ -ris,

Toi l'É-ter-nel ___, Ô Sei-gneur é-ter-nel !

We, verily, have made music as a ladder for your souls, a means whereby they may be lifted up unto the realm on high; make it not, therefore, as wings to self and passion.

Bahá'u'lláh, the Kitáb-i-Aqdas

O Be Joyful!

Sung as a three-part round
Text and Music: ?
Arrangement: Ruth Vander Stelt, 2000

O be joy-ful, O be ju-bi-lant, Put your sor-rows far a-way,

Come re-joice and sing to-ge-ther this

2.

hap-py day. O be joy-ful, O be

3.

joy-ful on this day. O be-joy ful, O be joy-ful,

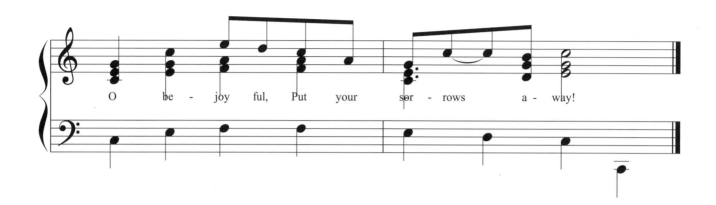

O be - joy ful, Put your sor - rows a - way!

Prayer for the Dead

Text: Bahá'u'lláh
Music: Ruth Vander Stelt, 2002

*The Prayer for the Dead is to be used for Bahá'ís over the age of
15. "It is the only Bahá'í obligatory prayer which is to be recited in
congregation; it is to be recited by one believer while all present
stand."*

— the Kitáb-i-Aqdas

*(If the dead be a woman, let him say: This is Thy handmaiden
and the daughter of Thy handmaiden, etc ...)Instructions and first
portion of this obligatory prayer are found*

O my God! This is Thy servant and the son of Thy servant who hath believed in Thee and in Thy
signs, and set his face towards Thee, wholly detached from all except Thee. Thou art, verily, of those
who show mercy the most merciful.

Deal with him, O Thou Who forgivest the sins of men and concealest their faults, as beseemeth the
heaven of Thy bounty and the ocean of Thy grace. Grant him admission within the precincts of Thy
transcendent mercy that was before the foundation of earth and heaven. There is no God butThee, the
Ever-Forgiving, the Most Generous.

Let him, then, repeat six times the greeting "Alláh'u'Abhá" *and then repeat nineteen times each of the
following verses:*

We all, verily, worship God... (see musical score)

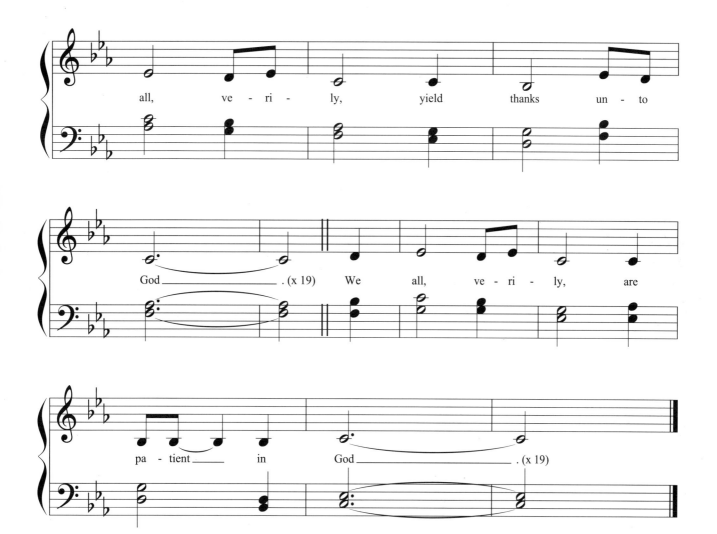

all, ve - ri - ly, yield thanks un - to

God_____ . (x 19) We all, ve - ri - ly, are

pa - tient_____ in God_____ . (x 19)

The Long Healing Prayer

The repetitive portion of the prayer is sung in simple harmony;
the rest is read by one or more people.
See page 146 for text of prayer
Text: Prayer by Bahá'u'lláh
Music and Arrangement: Ruth Vander Stelt, 1999

Thou the Suf- fi ___ cing, Thou the ___ Hea ___ ling, Thou the A - bi ___ ding,

O Thou A - bi - ding One!

180

Thy Name is my Healing

Text: Bahá'u'lláh
Music and Arrangement: Ruth Vander Stelt, 1998

Thy Name is my hea-ling O God____. Re-mem-brance of
Thee is my re____-me-dy, O God____. Near-ness to
Thee is my hope and love for Thee my com-pa-
nion, O God____. Thy Mer-cy to me is my hea-

ling   in   this world and   worlds   to   come.   Veri - ly art

Thou the all   Boun - ti - ful,   Ve __ - ri - ly,   All   Wise.

Veri - ly art   Thou the All   Know - ing,   Ve __ - ri

- ly   All   Wise _____

Appendix Two

Arabic Pronunciation Key
Index of First Lines
Audio References

Arabic Pronunciation Key

Arabic Pronunciation Key

a . . . . as in "account"

á . . . . as in "arm"

i . . . . as (e) in "best"

í . . . . as (ee) in "meet"

u . . . . as (o) in "short"

ú . . . . as (oo) in moon

aw . . as in "mown"

Examples:

'Abdu'l-Bahá . . . . . .ab-dol-ba-haw
Alláh'u'Abhá . . . . . .al-law-ho-ab-haw
Báb . . . . .bawb
Bahá'u'lláh . . . . .ba-haw-ol-law
Yá Bahá'ul-Abhá . . .yaw-ba-haw-ol-ab-haw

Index of First Lines

Audio References

Audio material from the following composers may be obtained using these coordinates:

Composer/Compositeur	Coordinates/Coordonnées
Andrea Graham	(613) 582-7091
Anis Mangenda	dweyers@global.co.za
Ariel Barkley	barkleys@bmts.com
Benjamin Dlamini	available on "Lift up your Voices", Vol 3, see Tom Price
Chantal Daigle	1525 Diefenbaker Court, App 313, Pickering, ON, L1V 3W1
Bijan Khadem-Missagh	"Call of the Beloved", Dawn Breakers, Bahá'í Haus, Thimiggasse 12, 1180 Vienna, Austria
Bill Staines	see Red Grammer's album, "Down the DoReMi"
Dick Grover	3458 S.E. Cora Dr., Portland, OR, 97202, (503) 736-9388, dijagro@teleport.com
Elizabeth Hahn	available on "Songs of the Ancient Beauty," see Tom Price
Jack Lenz	www.liveunity.com
Jim Styan	http://members.shaw.ca/bounties/
Josée Cardinal	unavailable
Joyce & Danny Deardorff	contact Marcia Day at: 3401 Batavia St., Nashville, Tennessee, 37209; mdaypavon@aol.com
Kathryn Tahiri	Celestial Navigation Music Publishing and Services, celnav@earthlink.net , 847-853-1294
Marg Raynor	see Ariel Barkley
Nancy Ward	n.ward@lycos.com
Patrick Arnaud	CD « Fais chanter ton cœur » available from the Librairie Bahá'íe, Paris - France, 45, rue Pergolèse, 75 116 Paris - France. Tél: +33 1 45 00 33 12. Fax: +33 1 45 00 05 79. E-mail: libahaie@club-internet.fr.
Red Grammer	Smilin' Atcha Music, Inc., P.O. Box 446, Chester, N.Y., (914) 469-9450
Ruth Vander Stelt	c/o the LSA of the Bahá'ís of Gatineau, C.P. 79033, Gatineau, Québec, J8Y 6V2, pamarsh@storm.ca
Tom Price	Global Music Inc., 134 Gatone Dr., Hendersonville, TN, 37075, Tel: (615) 822-1822, Fax: (615) 822-8720, tom.price@nashville.com
Suzanne Hébert	cassette, « Demain les enfants de la terre », available from Service de distribution bahá'í - Québec, sdbq.quebec@3web.net
Tim Urbonya	urbonya@merr.com
Wiley Rinaldi	see Nancy Ward

Notes

Notes

Notes

Notes

Notes